MW00943695

Developing Your Spiritual Eyesight

Insights From The New Testament Book of Ephesians

by

Mark Eaton

Copyright © 2011 Mark Eaton

All rights reserved.

First edition

Scripture quotations marked "NKJV™" are taken from the
New King James Version®. Copyright © 1982 by Thomas
Nelson, Inc. Used by permission. All rights reserved.

Scripture quotations marked (ESV) are from The Holy Bible,
English Standard Version® (ESV®), copyright © 2001 by
Crossway, a publishing ministry of Good News Publishers.
Used by permission. All rights reserved.

Scripture quotations marked (KJV) are from The Holy Bible,
King James Version, Public Domain.

ISBN-10: 1466333499
ISBN-13: 978-1466333499

DEDICATION

With gratitude to Jesus Christ,
my family
and
Porterfield Baptist Church
who have supported me in ministry
and the endeavor of writing this book.

.

CONTENTS

Introduction

This book is written as a study guide to help seekers and newer followers of Christ grow in their understanding and application of Scriptural principles found in the New Testament book of Ephesians. It is my hope that more mature followers of Christ will be encouraged by reading it as well. Though it is not intended to be a comprehensive commentary on the entirety of Ephesians, I hope it provides enough depth and insight to be helpful. I recommend having your Bible nearby to reference as you read this book.

As the apostle Paul prayed for the believers in Ephesus I also pray for each of you who engage in this study of Ephesians that the God and Father of our Lord Jesus Christ may give you the spirit of wisdom and revelation in the knowledge of Him.

Chapter 1

Recognizing What You Have

Insights from <u>Chapter One of Ephesians</u>

AN AMAZING DISCOVERY

In 2007 a man named George Brock and his wife Leslie were having lunch at a restaurant in South Florida. They decided to order some steamed clams which they normally don't eat. As Mr. Brock bit into one of the tender morsels his teeth struck something hard like a stone. He quickly spit it out on his plate thinking it was a piece of clamshell. After taking a closer look, he noticed that the hard thing he had bitten down on was not a piece of shell, but a pearl! This was no ordinary pearl, it was purple. A purple pearl is extremely rare and to come from the inside of a clam is even more unusual. Of course he kept this rare treasure. The couple took it to a jeweler who confirmed it was indeed authentic. The pearl was estimated to be worth several thousand dollars.

Imagine if Mr. Brock had not looked a little closer at what was on his plate. Imagine if he had just hastily and ignorantly thrown it away. He would have missed out on realizing the value of what he had in his possession. Fortunately for him, he took the time to examine what was in his mouth, and on his plate.

There are many people in the world today who don't realize the value of "the pearl" of Jesus Christ and the gospel message. Like Mr. Brock, when we make an unusual discovery, we need to take time to investigate the value of what we have discovered.

Under the leadership of God's Holy Spirit, the apostle Paul wrote to help the church of Ephesus better understand the value of their faith in Jesus. That's why Paul penned the following words about the importance of having proper spiritual understanding.

Ephesians 1:15-19 "NKJV™"
15 Therefore I also, after I heard of your faith in the Lord Jesus and your love for all the saints,
16 do not cease to give thanks for you, making mention of you in my prayers:
17 that the God of our Lord Jesus Christ, the Father of glory, may give to you the spirit of wisdom and revelation in the knowledge of Him,
18 the eyes of your understanding being enlightened; that you may know what is the hope of His calling, what are the riches of the glory of His inheritance in the saints,
19 and what is the exceeding greatness of His power toward us who believe.

In verse eighteen Paul mentions that he is praying for their spiritual understanding to become more clear. He uses the term "eyes" to indicate the ability to perceive. It is a spiritual perception; a spiritual eyesight. He identifies three profound aspects of that spiritual eyesight which every believer in Christ should become aware of. These three aspects become focal points for our spiritual eyes.

3

He mentions hope, riches and power. Who
wouldn't be interested in knowing more about
these? What kind of hope? What kind of riches?
What kind of power?

A LIVING HOPE

The first focal point Paul identifies with his
prayer in Ephesians 1:18 is the hope to which God is
calling us in Christ. The apostle Peter refers to this
same hope in 1 Peter 1:3 where he calls it a "living
hope." It is a living hope because it is placed in the
resurrected Son of God, Jesus Christ.

As we look closely at the first six verses of
Paul's letter to the Ephesians, we see him give a
preview for the basis of this hope we have.

Ephesians 1:1-6 (KJV)
1 Paul, an apostle of Jesus Christ by the will of God, to the
saints which are at Ephesus, and to the faithful in Christ Jesus:
2 Grace be to you, and peace, from God our Father, and from
the Lord Jesus Christ.
3 Blessed be the God and Father of our Lord Jesus Christ,
who hath blessed us with all spiritual blessings in heavenly
places in Christ:
4 According as he hath **chosen** us in him before the
foundation of the world, that we should be holy and without
blame before him in love:
5 Having **predestinated** us unto the **adoption** of children by
Jesus Christ to himself, according to the good pleasure of his
will,
6 To the praise of the glory of his grace, wherein he hath made
us **accepted** in the beloved.

4

In addressing this letter "to the saints" who are in Ephesus, Paul is not referring to some elite group of believers. He is referring to all who are genuinely trusting in Jesus for the forgiveness of sins, and who are yielding their lives to Him by faith. He refers to them as "the faithful in Jesus Christ." In other writings of the New Testament Paul uses the term "saints" in reference to followers of Christ Jesus. Some of these many references can be found in the following passages: 1 Corinthians 1:2; 2 Corinthians 1:1; Philippians 1:1; Colossians 1:2; and Hebrews 13:24. As modern day faithful followers of Jesus Christ, we also are part of this group that has been growing through history.

Paul wants us to realize that through Christ we have peace with God and continuous spiritual blessings. These blessings include adoption into God's family by His grace and good will. The hope of peace and blessing we have in Christ is so sure that Paul used four expressive words to help us understand God's love and purpose for us. In Christ Jesus we are "chosen," "predestined," "adopted," and "accepted" by God. All four of these words show us concepts that describe God as the One who takes the initiative in bringing us into a relationship with Himself. It is not based on our goodness or ability, but solely on God's grace. The reality is, if God did not intervene in your life, there would be no way that you could know Him or enter into a personal relationship with Him. God has made it His choice. This is a wonderful concept!

You may not have been chosen for the school team you wanted to be on. You may not have been chosen by the college you wanted to attend. You may have been rejected by that special person you wanted to date. You may not have been chosen for that job position that you were hoping for, but before the world was created, God had you in mind, and He chose you in Christ Jesus and predestined you to be accepted and adopted as His child! God makes it clear through His word that He has done this by His own purpose, His love and His grace. This is a sure hope we can trust in! This is the hope to which God has called you. This is a living hope because it is placed in our living Savior and Lord, Jesus Christ!

A RICH INHERITANCE

The second focal point mentioned in Ephesians 1:18 that Paul wants us to direct our spiritual eyes toward is "the riches of his glorious inheritance in the saints". Being a follower of Christ is not easy. As we face the trials and difficulties of everyday living, it helps to know that our faith in Christ is not in vain, and not without rewards as we stay faithful. There is a wealth of God's grace that is available to help us through this life. There is also a great inheritance we can benefit from now and look forward to in the future. Paul introduces the concept of this inheritance in Ephesians 1:9-14 .

Ephesians 1:9-14 (KJV)
9 Having made known unto us the mystery of his will, according to his good pleasure which he hath purposed in himself:
10 That in the dispensation of the fulness of times he might gather together in one all things in Christ, both which are in heaven, and which are on earth; even in him:
11 In whom also we have obtained an **inheritance**, being predestinated according to the purpose of him who worketh all things after the counsel of his own will:
12 That we should be to the praise of his glory, who first trusted in Christ.
13 In whom ye also trusted, after that ye heard the word of truth, the gospel of your salvation: in whom also after that ye believed, ye were sealed with that holy Spirit of promise,
14 Which is the earnest of our **inheritance** until the redemption of the purchased possession, unto the praise of his glory.

Notice Paul refers to an "inheritance" in verses eleven and fourteen as well as verse eighteen of chapter one. The actual Greek word Paul used in the text is *kleronomia* which means "that which is given to one as a possession that has either been received or will be received." [1] The riches of an inheritance are not normally received until the owner of the inheritance dies. When Jesus Christ died on the cross, God granted inheritance rights and the spiritual riches of Christ to all who trust Him as Savior. Because Jesus conquered death and arose back to life, believers can enjoy the promise and benefits of this inheritance with Him now and forever.

Through the riches of God's grace (His kindness toward unworthy sinners) He provides an inheritance of forgiveness through the blood of Jesus Christ. Paul tells us in Ephesians 1:7-8 that in Christ we have redemption and forgiveness of sins according to the riches of His grace. The apostle John confirms this concept in 1 John 1:8-9.

1 John 1:8-9 (KJV)
8 If we say that we have no sin, we deceive ourselves, and the truth is not in us.
9 If we confess our sins, he is faithful and just to forgive us our sins, and to cleanse us from all unrighteousness.

---

[1]Strong, James: *The Exhaustive Concordance of the Bible : Showing Every Word of the Test of the Common English Version of the Canonical Books, and Every Occurence of Each Word in Regular Order.* electronic ed. Ontario : Woodside Bible Fellowship., 1996, S. H0

These verses contain a promise from God. If we admit our guilt of sins to God in all sincerity, trusting in what Jesus Christ has done for us, we will not only be forgiven for what we have done wrong, but we will also be given a clean record in God's sight! The basis for the assurance of this forgiveness is found in the person and work of Jesus Christ alone. This is part of the rich inheritance we can share in. We are rich in forgiveness from God.

This concept is summarized in 2 Corinthians 5:21. Paul states that God appointed Jesus Christ, who never sinned, to be the offering for our sin, so that we could be made right with God through Him.

Think of it this way. Our sin has put us in a tremendous debt toward the holiness and righteousness of God's character. None of us have the moral or spiritual capacity to repay that debt. Though we may try by various means to reconcile the debt and be acceptable to God through our own efforts, it is impossible. Knowing this, God provides the resources by His grace through the second person of His own Triune being – Jesus Christ. The righteousness of Christ and His atoning blood poured out at Calvary are the only forms of spiritual currency that are adequate to satisfy this debt we owe to God.

When Jesus willingly gave His life on the cross for us, He was paying the debt to God that we owe.

He was also securing our inheritance in Him. When we personally confess our sin debt and receive Jesus into our lives it is as if in a spiritual sense, the full and perfect righteousness of Christ is credited to our spiritual bank account. Through faith in Christ's payment to God for us, we are made right with God. Our spiritual bank statement so to speak is reconciled with God. We not only have a balanced account, we have a surplus of Christ's righteousness credited to our account. The result is that we can have a positive relationship with God and dwell in His presence and blessing forever. That's a rich inheritance that we share with other believers or "saints" as Paul refers to them.

Christ's sacrifice to God on our behalf has redeemed us from the curse of sin and death that separates us from God. As Paul proclaims in Romans 6:23, "The wages of sin is death; but the gift of God is eternal life through Jesus Christ our Lord." Because Jesus conquered death through His resurrection, we anticipate a resurrection for us also by His power.

As we study other passages of the New Testament we find that the riches of this glorious inheritance include a wonderful new type of resurrected body in which we will able to share eternal life and health with Jesus Christ (see 1 Cor. 15:35-58). This inheritance also includes living in a glorious new heaven and earth community, in perfect harmony with God and each other.

We get a glimpse of this inheritance from the view of revelation given to the apostle John who was one of Jesus' closest disciples. It is recorded in Revelation chapter 21.

Revelation 21:1-8 "NKJV™"

1 Now I saw a new heaven and a new earth, for the first heaven and the first earth had passed away. Also there was no more sea.

2 Then I, John, saw the holy city, New Jerusalem, coming down out of heaven from God, prepared as a bride adorned for her husband.

3 And I heard a loud voice from heaven saying, "Behold, the tabernacle of God is with men, and He will dwell with them, and they shall be His people. God Himself will be with them and be their God.

4 And God will wipe away every tear from their eyes; there shall be no more death, nor sorrow, nor crying. There shall be no more pain, for the former things have passed away."

5 Then He who sat on the throne said, "Behold, I make all things new." And He said to me, "Write, for these words are true and faithful."

6 And He said to me, "It is done! I am the Alpha and the Omega, the Beginning and the End. I will give of the fountain of the water of life freely to him who thirsts.

7 He who overcomes shall inherit all things, and I will be his God and he shall be My son.

8 But the cowardly, unbelieving, abominable, murderers, sexually immoral, sorcerers, idolaters, and all liars shall have their part in the lake which burns with fire and brimstone, which is the second death."

In this Revelation passage and throughout the Bible, there is both encouragement and warning. That's why it is imperative to look at life from God's eternal perspective. We can do this by prayerfully studying His Word and by the spiritual insight that He gives us through the direction of His Holy Spirit.

Notice once again the word "inherit" in verse seven. It is the same Greek word that the Holy Spirit guided the apostle Paul to use in Ephesians. Since God prompted the early apostles to mention this inheritance in several different writings, it must be important. God wants you to understand what you have available to you through His promises in Christ Jesus. That is why Paul made it one of his focal points of prayer, asking God to help us know the riches of this glorious inheritance.

Take a few moments now to reflect on what you understand of the spiritual riches that are accessible to you through Jesus Christ. Do you understand the riches of His forgiveness available to you? Is there some sin that you need to confess to Him? Take the opportunity now to confess and receive His forgiveness and spiritual cleansing.

How does knowing about this inheritance in Christ help you see yourself in comparison to circumstances you are facing right now in your life? What aspects of this inheritance are you enjoying now and what are you looking forward to enjoying in the future?

POWER FOR US WHO BELIEVE

The third focal point we need to envision with our spiritual eyes is described by Paul in Ephesians 1:19 as God's incomparably great power for us who believe. Paul included praying for our ability to see and know the power we have available to us from Christ because we face spiritual opposition every day. We are in a spiritual war with the forces and influences of Satan in the world. Paul addresses this topic further toward the end of his letter in Ephesians chapter six. Satan works against us in blatant and subtle ways to discourage our faith. It is only through the power of Christ's Holy Spirit at work within us and on our behalf that we can become fully aware of this opposition and overcome it. Understanding the power that Jesus Christ provides for us helps us not get discouraged when we face difficulties in life. Paul elaborates in Ephesians 1:19-23 about this power which he prays we will begin to understand more fully. Let's look at the passage in context:

Ephesians 1:15-23 (KJV)
15 Wherefore I also, after I heard of your faith in the Lord Jesus, and love unto all the saints,
16 Cease not to give thanks for you, making mention of you in

13

my prayers;

17 That the God of our Lord Jesus Christ, the Father of glory, may give unto you the spirit of wisdom and revelation in the knowledge of him:

18 The eyes of your understanding being enlightened; that ye may know what is the hope of his calling, and what the riches of the glory of his inheritance in the saints,

19 And what is the exceeding greatness of his **power(1)** to us-ward who believe, according to the **working(2)** of his **mighty(3) power(4),**

20 Which he **wrought(5)** in Christ, when he raised him from the dead, and set him at his own right hand in the heavenly places,

21 Far above all principality, and power, and might, and dominion, and every name that is named, not only in this world, but also in that which is to come:

22 And hath put all things under his feet, and gave him to be the head over all things to the church,

23 Which is his body, the fulness of him that filleth all in all.

The concept of Christ's power being available to help us is so important that Paul enlisted five different words from the Greek vocabulary to get this point across. In the passage just presented I have emphasized and numbered these five words and provided clarification for each corresponding numbered word in the following ways:

1) Power - In the first half of verse nineteen Paul uses the Greek word "dunamis" which is translated into English with the word, "power". Dunamis means inherent power residing in something by virtue of its nature. It is the power which a

person or thing exerts and puts forth. This Greek word is used in the New Testament to refer to the power to perform miracles or of a moral power and excellence of soul. Strong's Exhaustive Concordance of the Bible and Enhanced Lexicon [2] points out that it has other nuances which give us a better understanding of the word. Dunamis can mean the power and influence which belong to riches and wealth. It can refer to the power and resources arising from numbers such as the power consisting in or resting upon armies or multitudes.

Our English terms "dynamo" and "dynamite" come from this Greek word. Dunamis, dynamo and dynamite are all words with powerful imagery to help us see the power from God which is available to us!

2) Working - The Greek word translated as "working" which Paul uses in verse nineteen is "energeia." It means a strong, effectual and efficient power at work. This Greek word is where our English word "energy" comes from, but the energy that is being referenced in this passage and wherever it is used in the New Testament is talking about superhuman power. A power beyond ourselves. It is this kind of power that God will use to raise us from the dead. It is

---

[2]Strong, James: *The Exhaustive Concordance of the Bible : Showing Every Word of the Test of the Common English Version of the Canonical Books, and Every Occurence of Each Word in Regular Order.* electronic ed. Ontario : Woodside Bible Fellowship., 1996, S. H0

the kind of power God directs toward us and in us when we need it most!

3) Mighty - The Greek word translated into English as "mighty" in verse nineteen is "ischus." This Greek word places the emphasis on the strength and ability that resides within a person or being ready to be unleashed. It gives the impression of a force to be reckoned with.

4) Power - The second time in verse nineteen that the English word "power" appears actually comes from a different Greek word than the first one used in this verse. The Greek word Paul used here in the verse is "kratos." This word is used to describe a mighty deed done as a work of dominion. It is a work of power as a result of the might within. It gives the picture of being able to overcome any resistance. This also is the power God directs on our behalf to accomplish His will.

5) Wrought - In verse twenty Paul uses the Greek word "energeo" that is translated into English as "wrought" or "worked." This Greek word means to put forth power or display work in operation. Paul is describing here the tremendous power of God at work in the body of Jesus Christ when He was raised from the dead.

The Holy Spirit inspired Paul to use some great word pictures. Ephesians 1:19-23 describes the divine, dynamic, eternal energy and power available to help us through God's Holy Spirit! Though this power is available to us and working on our behalf, it comes at the discretion of God. It cannot be used by our own manipulative efforts or through some routine formula. It is both real and miraculous. It is put into effect as we live by faith in Christ Jesus. This power includes the ability to persevere through the difficult circumstances in life. It involves the power of His Holy Spirit working through us to help others. It includes the power to live by the new nature that Christ puts within us that results in love, joy, peace, patience, kindness, goodness, gentleness and self control in increasing measure (See Galatians 5:22-23). It includes the power to resist temptation and sinful practices that harm us and are displeasing to God. It includes power for healing. It includes the power by which at a future time God will give to us new glorified resurrected bodies fit for eternal life!

By receiving Christ as our Savior and yielding our lives over to Him in full submission of our will to His, He works in and through us by the power and person of His Holy Spirit.

What good is hope if you don't persevere in it? What good is power if you don't realize you have it? What good are riches if you don't know how to use them? What benefit is your hope, power and wealth in Christ to others if you won't put them to good use? The life of Henrietta Green is a sad and true example of a person not using available resources to make life better for themselves or others.

THE STORY OF HENRIETTA GREEN

Henrietta "Hetty" Green was the richest woman in the United States one hundred years ago. She died in 1916 at the age of eighty one. When she died, her fortune was estimated at one hundred million dollars. That would be the equivalent of at least one and a half billion dollars by today's standards! Yet during her life-time she lived like a poor person.

At times she lived in a series of grungy leased rooms, spending as little as five dollars a week for living expenses. She would buy broken cookies in bulk because they were cheaper than whole ones. She wore the same black dress day after day until it wore out. When she absolutely had to wash the garment, she often instructed that it be laundered only on the bottom where it was dirty in order to save money for cleaning costs.

When her son Ned was fourteen years old, he dislocated his knee in a sledding mishap. Though Hetty had enough wealth to take him to the finest medical facilities and physicians in the world, she refused to take him to a hospital. Instead she tried to treat the injury at home and by visiting free clinics. Eventually because of her son not getting the care he could have received with the money she had, gangrene set in and Ned's leg had to be amputated.

Her miserly ways, her black dress, her shrewd investing principles and her time living in New York earned her the nickname, "The Witch of Wall Street." Because of her wealth she spent her last few years in fear of being kidnapped or killed though there were no known threats. When Hetty Green died she left her entire fortune to her son Ned, and her daughter, who decided to use and enjoy what they had been given!

THE POINT OF THE STORY

God wants you to realize the hope, rich inheritance and power you have in Christ. Don't be stingy like Henrietta Green when it comes to using the resources which God has made available to you.

Why has God the father chosen us, adopted us, predestined us, and accepted us in Christ Jesus? Why has God the Son redeemed us, forgiven us, revealed God's will to us, and made us part of God's inheritance? Why has God the Spirit sealed us and become the guarantee of our future blessing? Paul tells us in Ephesians 1:12-14 that God has done all these things "to the praise of His glory!" This means that God wants us to let other people know what He offers, and help them come to know the love and goodness of God by reflecting His love and grace through Christ's Holy Spirit working in us!

God does all of this for the praise of His glory, and He wants us to have the spiritual eyes to see it. His creation reveals His wisdom and power. His son Jesus Christ reveals His love and grace. His Holy Spirit empowers, teaches and enlightens us. That's how Paul wrote the letter to the Ephesians and why I am writing this book. Do you see the value of what you have available to you?

REALIZING WHAT WE HAVE

Like the pearl from a clam in Mr. Brock's mouth, though he did not expect it or deserve it, when he was made aware of it, he kept it, checked its value, and is enjoying the wealth of it! In another letter Paul wrote to believers in Rome, he describes a similar dynamic of how close the Word of God is to us. Paul says in Romans 10:8 that the word of God is near us. Near enough to be in our mouth and in our heart. What we need to do is become aware of it, check its value, and apply it to our lives through faith in Jesus Christ.

You cannot deserve or earn these spiritual riches which Paul writes about; you can only receive them by God's grace, through faith in Christ. If you have not received Jesus Christ as Savior, I pray you will. I pray that the eyes of your heart may be enlightened. If you have trusted Jesus as Savior, I pray that you may know the hope to which he has called you, the riches of his glorious inheritance in the saints, and his incomparably great power for us who believe.

SOME THINGS TO THINK ABOUT

Take a few moments now to reflect on God's power that He works toward you and in you as you believe in Christ. Look again at the five descriptive words for power mentioned in Ephesians 1:19-20 along with the descriptions for each Greek word on pages 14-16 of this book. How have you experienced His power in your life in each of those ways? In what ways do you trust to see His power at work in your life in the future? How does this motivate you to live differently? How will you use this power to help others?

Chapter 2
Seeing Yourself from God's Perspective

Insights from Chapter Two of Ephesians

FAILURE OR FORTUNE ?

A chemist named Spencer Silver was trying to develop a strong adhesive in the 3M research laboratories during 1968. He was curious about what would happen if he mixed an unusual amount of monomers into a polymer-based adhesive he was working on. The result was a new adhesive that instead of being very strong was very weak. It was only tacky enough to hold two sheets of paper together, but it could easily be removed without leaving any residue on the paper. Though Spencer told others in the company about his discovery, no one realized the usefulness for an adhesive that would not stick very well. Regardless of his discouragement, Silver kept his research notes and the adhesive.

A few years later in 1974, another 3M colleague named Arthur Fry was singing in his church choir. He became frustrated because the slips of paper he placed in his hymnal to identify songs they were going to sing would sometimes slide out and fall to the floor, causing him to lose his place, (not to mention some embarrassment.) Then he remembered the "useless" adhesive that his co-workers at 3M had talked about a few years earlier.

When Mr. Fry went back to work he asked Spencer Silver about the adhesive. Upon getting a sample of it, he used some to coat his paper markers.

It worked perfectly for his application! With the weak adhesive, the markers stayed in place, yet could be lifted off without damaging the pages in the song book. Then an idea was birthed to use the glue on paper note pads so that notes could be detached and stuck on anything as reminders.

3M began distributing Post-it® Notes nationwide in 1980 -- twelve years after Spencer developed the weak adhesive. After only two years on the market, the little sticky notes became a best seller for office supplies, and the product is now a part of our everyday lives.

People may have seen Spencer Silver as a failure for a brief time after his initial experiment, but God used a man singing in a church choir and Spencer's "mistake" to show the 3M Company how valuable his discovery really was.

There may be times when we see ourselves as failures. We may feel we are somewhat useless to God and His church, but Paul says because of what Jesus Christ has accomplished for us and offers to us, he can take the failures of our lives and turn them into something of great worth. Through faith in Christ we go from failure to fortune! Christ can take what you perceive as a weakness in your personality and turn it into a great asset for His Kingdom.

That's why Paul prayed that as believers in Christ we would have crystal clear spiritual eyesight.

We learned in Ephesians 1:18-19 that we need to keep our spiritual eyes directed at three focal points. These were detailed in chapter one. First we need to focus on the hope to which God has called us in Christ. Second, we need to become aware of the riches of His glorious inheritance in the saints. And third we need to realize His incomparably great power for us who believe.

WHO YOU ARE WITHOUT CHRIST

Paul continues to write under the inspiration of God's Holy Spirit in Ephesians chapter two so that our spiritual eyesight can be developed. Once again he uses authoritative imagery in verses one through three to help us see ourselves from God's perspective. Very bluntly he states that without Christ we are spiritually "dead" in our trespasses and sins. We are unable to understand and appreciate the true spiritual things of God. We are separated from the spiritual life that God offers. Paul also points out that before receiving Christ we are vulnerable, living under Satan's influence in the world whether we realize it or not. In Ephesians 2:3 Paul further details the effects of living under that sway by saying we were gratifying the cravings of our sinful nature and following its desires and thoughts. Advertising and marketing phrases we have heard over the years such as "Have it your way;" "No rules, just right;" and "Indulge yourself;" all appeal to that part of our nature that desires constant pleasure. It's not that God wants us to be denied of every pleasure in life, but when we live by the control of our sin nature, no pleasure is ever enough.

Under the cravings of our sin nature we are constantly in search of the newest thing that we can do or be involved in to find pleasure apart from God. When we reject finding pleasure primarily in a relationship with God who loves us and gives us life, we are unwittingly placing ourselves in league with Satan. As such, Paul points out in verse three that we are living as "children of wrath". That means from God's holy perspective we are under His judgment against Satan and sinful rebellion. Holiness and sinfulness are like oil and water. They don't mix! We remain under God's judgment against sin and unrighteousness in the world until we receive the way out from under it which He has provided through His Son.

People without Jesus Christ in their life may think they are okay. They may think they look right to God, but He sees things differently. Have you ever been in a conversation with someone when you noticed that they had a piece of food stuck between their teeth? They continue to talk, smile and laugh but are totally unaware of that disturbing sight you are trying not to stare at. You don't want to embarrass them, but you also want them to be aware so they can take care of the distraction. At first they may not appreciate you pointing out the problem, but if they realize the further embarrassment you have saved them from, they will be glad you did. Experiencing this also reminds us to take a look at ourselves in the mirror on a regular basis!

In a similar way many people go through their days unaware of the sins in their life that are so apparent to God and even to others. James 1:22-25 tells us that the written Word of God in the Bible is a spiritual mirror that we can use to make us aware of things in our life that are not right in God's sight which need to be corrected. It may be unpleasant and emotionally painful to see at times, but we need to be attentive. Once we realize the problem we can ask God for help in making appropriate changes.

Paul identifies some specific aspects of the sin nature in Galatians 5:19-21 that are displeasing to God. This is not an all inclusive list but it helps us see from God's perspective. Paul lists the following characteristics as manifestations of our sin nature; sexual immorality, impurity, dishonesty, idolatry, witchcraft, hatred, discord, jealousy, uncontrolled rage, envy, strife and drunkenness to name a few. Galatians 5:21 ends with a strong warning that "they

which do such things shall not inherit the Kingdom
of God."

We are warned several times in the New
Testament that unless we are changed by the Spirit
of God through faith in Jesus Christ and the work of
His Holy Spirit in our lives, we will not be able to
dwell in God's presence in Heaven, or be part of His
Kingdom here on earth.

1 Corinthians 6:9-11 (KJV)
9 Know ye not that the unrighteous shall not inherit the
kingdom of God? Be not deceived: neither fornicators, nor
idolaters, nor adulterers, nor effeminate, nor abusers of
themselves with mankind,
10 Nor thieves, nor covetous, nor drunkards, nor revilers, nor
extortioners, shall inherit the kingdom of God.
11 And such were some of you: but ye are washed, but ye are
sanctified, but ye are justified in the name of the Lord Jesus,
and by the Spirit of our God.

This is a difficult passage in the light of God's
grace, but we can't ignore it. Paul reminds us that
before we trusted Christ as Savior we were separated
from God and His Kingdom. We were each caught
up in the various thoughts and acts of the sinful
nature with the rest of fallen humanity. But after
receiving Christ and His Holy Spirit, we now have
His power available to us and working in us so that
we can live differently than the way we used to. We
don't have to give in to the strong pull of those

desires. Though we were living by our sinful cravings before we surrendered to Christ by faith, we are reminded in 2 Corinthians 5:17 that now in Christ we are a new creation with His power available to us. The old has gone, and a new life has begun! God's grace creates in us a new nature in the power of His Holy Spirit. This reinforces the need for us to see with our spiritual eyes His incomparably great power for us who believe.

1 Corinthians 6:9-11 as well as Ephesians 2:1-3 are not describing trying to be a better person by your own power. Those passages describe the need to trust in the finished work of Christ to provide forgiveness for all of your sins, past, present and future, as well as a reliance on His Holy Spirit's power to help you live by the new nature God puts within you.

Paul cautions us to remember who we were before Christ came into our life. This keeps us from becoming conceited or arrogant in dealing with others who have not yet come to Christ. It is also a warning for us not to continue in yielding to the old desires or going back to them.

WHO YOU ARE WITH CHRIST

Paul transitions next in Ephesians 2:4-10 to help us see from God's perspective who we are *with* Jesus in our lives. Once again Paul uses potent metaphors to help us realize the difference Christ makes in us. It helps to personalize these verses. Verse five tells you in Christ, you are made spiritually alive. Through the power of Christ's Holy Spirit at work inside of your soul, he has now given you spiritual life that you did not have before. Because of this new spiritual birth you are able to begin to see things from God's perspective in a way that you were not able to see before. This spiritual life also now connects you with God through Christ and prepares you for eternal life in fellowship and harmony with Him.

Verse six tells you that with Christ in your life you are "seated together in heavenly places in Christ Jesus." To understand what this phrase means, consider the following example.

An elected officer has an official seat or position that he or she occupies when they serve in their capacity at meetings. That elected official still holds the position of authority or responsibility even though they journey from place to place. They are the only one who is officially recognized to sit in their particular chair of leadership. As they travel about and do their work, their position in relation to their office is maintained. So it is with we who have received Jesus Christ and are seated with Christ in "heavenly places". We are not there yet, but we can operate in our capacity knowing the position is there! We are no longer only citizens of earth, but we are citizens of Heaven with a special place reserved for us in Christ Jesus and a special work that we are to do for His Kingdom and His glory!

WHO GOD CREATED YOU TO BE

That brings us to the phrase in verse ten, "we are his workmanship." Take a few moments to reflect on this and personalize it. In Christ you are a masterpiece of God's design for His specific purposes. He has created you in Christ Jesus for good works, which God prepared in advance that you should do for His Kingdom and His glory!

God has put within you certain abilities, spiritual gifts and talents that He wants you to use in order to help others come to know Him. Paul explains it further in chapter four of this letter to the Ephesians. It is amazing to see how God can take skills and abilities that we have and put them to use for His Kingdom even though we didn't think there was any connection or application where they could be used. We often look at the strengths and gifts of others, and assume if we don't have those particular abilities or talents, then we are useless to God. When you have those thoughts you need to look at a Post-it® Note and remember the illustration. Like Spencer Silver's weak adhesive which turned out to be a tremendously useful item, God can use our unnoticed abilities and personalities to bless others and build them up in faith in Christ by His power working through us.

As we read Ephesians 2:11-18 we see that Paul repeats his instructions to remember who we were without Christ and realize who we are with Christ. He goes on to explain that with Jesus Christ in our lives we need to see ourselves from God's perspective as part of a much bigger spiritual family. True faith in Jesus as Savior unites people from all different kinds of backgrounds into one new body of believers under the new covenant with God through the blood of His Son, Jesus.

Ephesians 2:19-22 "NKJV™"
19 Now, therefore, you are no longer strangers and foreigners, but fellow citizens with the saints and members of the household of God,
20 having been built on the foundation of the apostles and prophets, Jesus Christ Himself being the chief cornerstone,
21 in whom the whole building, being fitted together, grows into a holy temple in the Lord,
22 in whom you also are being built together for a dwelling place of God in the Spirit.

God wants you to see yourself as a part of something bigger than yourself! When you become a born again believer in Jesus Christ, you are part of the "one body" (Eph. 2:16) of Christ – in His church. You are part of His hands to help others in the world. You are part of His feet to go where He wants you to go. You are part of His mouth to speak His word. You are part of His arms to embrace others with His strength and love. You are part of His heartbeat of compassion in the world today! Jesus told us as we go throughout the world we are to encourage others to come to Him, receive Him into their lives and learn from Him. (Matthew 28:18-20). This is how we glorify God.

In Ephesians 2:19 Paul helps us see ourselves as one of the "fellow citizens" in Christ's Kingdom, and as "members of the household of God." He points out that as followers of Christ we are no longer strangers or foreigners to God. The word "stranger" in verse nineteen means an outsider, an unknown person, or a person who does not belong. The word "foreigner" means a migrant or an exile. Paul is showing us the contrast between a life without Christ and one with Christ. He is helping us develop our spiritual eyesight to see ourselves from God's perspective.

To believers Paul is saying in effect, "Remember who you were without Christ and recognize now who you are with Him in your life!" Remember there was a time when you were foreign to God and His kingdom, but now in Jesus Christ you are a fellow citizen. You are part of a new nation and society of God. God has given you spiritual rights and privileges as a citizen in His Kingdom. He wants you to learn how to live and thrive in His Kingdom.

Look at the phrase "of the household of God" in verse nineteen. With Jesus Christ in your life, you are now part of God's family. This also involves some wonderful privileges. Paul describes one of those privileges as adoption. Through faith in Jesus Christ you have been adopted as a child of God. You are considered as His son or His daughter and part of His family. All the experiences of God's family are now yours. This includes His love, care, interest, concern, provision, protection, instruction, discipline, and training.

As part of God's family you also have the privilege of responsibility and service. Yes, responsibility and service are actually privileges that can be enjoyed! In healthy families, every person of the household has duties to perform for the overall good of the family. We are responsible to love and help each other in order to strengthen the family of God.

What are you doing to contribute to God's family? There is no role that is too small to be important. When you pray for someone else, you are doing your part. When you help someone who is struggling you are doing your part. Paul points out a little later in his letter some specific ways we can do our part to help the family of God stay healthy and grow. Some of these examples are detailed in Ephesians chapter four.

As referenced earlier in Galatians 5:19-26 Paul contrasts the characteristics of those who are living outside of the family of God with the qualities of people who have been born into the family of God. Those outside of God's family are producing what Paul calls "works of the flesh." Those inside God's family learn to live by the power of His Holy Spirit at work in them which produces the "fruit of the Spirit."

Galatians 5:19-21 (ESV)
19 Now **the works of the flesh** are evident: sexual immorality, impurity, sensuality,
20 idolatry, sorcery, enmity, strife, jealousy, fits of anger, rivalries, dissensions, divisions,
21 envy, drunkenness, orgies, and things like these. I warn you, as I warned you before, that those who do such things will not inherit the kingdom of God.
22 But **the fruit of the Spirit** is love, joy, peace, patience, kindness, goodness, faithfulness,
23 gentleness, self-control; against such things there is no law.
24 And those who belong to Christ Jesus have crucified the flesh with its passions and desires.
25 If we live by the Spirit, let us also walk by the Spirit.

SOMETHING TO THINK ABOUT

As you look at Galatians 5:19-25, which characteristics listed in that passage are mostly at work in your life? This will help you see yourself from God's perspective. Ask for His help to change you accordingly.

Fish swim and birds fly because of their nature. They are born with the potential of their abilities. Those abilities are encoded in their DNA, but they still have to grow and develop them. When a person receives Jesus Christ into his or her life and is born again, Christ's Spirit enables them to live lives of love, joy, peace, patience, kindness, goodness, faithfulness, gentleness and self-control. As children of God we need to develop and practice these qualities implanted by the Holy Spirit. The point Paul is making is this; If you are a child of God, learn to live like one! Learn to use and develop the qualities His Holy Spirit has placed within you in ways that honor God.

IMPORTANT PARTS OF A BIGGER PICTURE

In Ephesians 2:21-22 Paul uses the analogy of building blocks in a temple of worship to help us see ourselves from God's perspective. He describes each of us who trust in Jesus Christ as a building block in God's house which He is putting together. The church is pictured as an ever expanding building. Each new believer in Christ is like a block or a brick added to the Lord's temple where His Spirit dwells. As Christ's Spirit indwells us, we are part of His living temple. God's Spirit is adding more and more believers each day as the gospel is spread and people respond by faith in Christ. The building grows and will continue to grow until the Lord Jesus Christ returns. You may not feel like you are anyone special but you are an important part of God's building connected and contributing to the whole!

If you are reading this and you don't have Jesus Christ in your life you need to understand that you are not a part of that building yet. You are spiritually dead, controlled by your sin nature, under the influence of Satan's power and still under God's wrath toward that which isn't right with Him.

The good news is, you don't have to stay that way. Come to Jesus. The fact that you are still reading this book indicates God's Spirit is working in your mind, heart and soul. Humble yourself before Him and ask Him to forgive you of your sins. Invite His Holy Spirit to come into your heart and life today. Ask God to adopt you into His family and give you true spiritual life. Ask Him to help you see life from His perspective and to help you live for Him from now on. With Christ in your life you can be a very important part of the living building he is putting together for His glory!

If you have Christ in your life then you are already a citizen in His Kingdom, a building block in His temple, a member of His family and a part of His body with a work that He wants you to do for His glory to help others know Him!

People didn't realize the value of Spencer Silver's weak adhesive until they saw it from Arthur Fry's perspective. Out of what most people viewed as a failure came a discovery of great worth. God wants you to see yourself from His perspective. He can use even your perceived weaknesses in ways you never imagined possible to touch people's lives in a positive way, but you have to surrender your life and will to His. He wants to use you in significant ways. Is your spiritual vision getting any clearer?

Chapter 3
Understanding The Mystery Of Messiah

Insights from <u>Chapter Three of Ephesians</u>

WHAT IS A MYSTERY?

A mystery is a secret, a riddle, or a puzzle which is presented in such a way that invites people to engage their minds to try and understand or solve the mystery. The elements of a mystery include some kind of dilemma, various clues regarding the situation and a resolution or conclusion. Most people enjoy mysteries because they challenge our thinking.

Without proper spiritual eyesight, God's plan and purpose for us through Jesus Christ remains a mystery. We can become confused by various religions and philosophies of the world and miss out on a true relationship with God.

In Ephesians chapter one, verse nine, the apostle Paul writes that God has revealed to us the mystery of His will according to His good pleasure, which He purposed in Christ. Paul mentions this mystery again in Ephesians chapter three. He says it is a mystery God has kept secret from the world until the time of Jesus Christ. This mystery contains all the classic elements. It includes a dilemma, some clues and a conclusion.

Let's see if we can use our spiritual eyesight to figure out this mystery together. Carefully read Ephesians 3:1-9. What is this mystery and how has it been revealed?

MYSTERY OF THE MESSIAH

Christ is the title for Messiah in the Greek language. Therefore the "mystery of Christ" that Paul mentions in verse four of this passage can also be called the mystery of the Messiah. Messiah means "anointed one." Old Testament prophecy was specifically pointing to the anointed one whom God would send into the world to usher in God's Kingdom Rule on earth.

Before Messiah entered the world, the nation of Israel wondered, "Who will He be? What exactly will He do? How will He relate to the nation of Israel? How will He relate to the rest of the world? How can non-Jewish people (Gentiles) and Jewish people live under the same rule of Messiah?" This presented a dilemma in their minds.

People outside of Israel were faced with another dilemma in their minds. How can a holy and righteous God forgive sinners and maintain His justice? How can God be loving and punish people for sin at the same time?

God gave many clues about this dilemma to the prophets of the Old Testament times, but even they didn't fully understand the mystery. It wasn't until after Jesus of Nazareth was miraculously born, grew to manhood, taught God's Word clearly, displayed God's power through healing and miracles, prophesied of the future, died on the cross, rose from the dead, ascended back to Heaven, and sent His Holy Spirit on the day of Pentecost, that the Jewish apostles began to understand these clues and the mystery of the Messiah more fully. (That's a lot of clues.) They were witnessing how Jesus was fulfilling the Old Testament prophecies about Messiah and began to realize that Jesus of Nazareth is indeed this promised Messiah!

As God's Holy Spirit spread to the nation of Israel and to people of other nationalities, the mystery of Messiah continued to be revealed. It is now reaching its conclusion through His church. Gentiles as well as Jewish people by faith in Christ are "fellow heirs" of all of God's promises in the work of Messiah on our behalf. The nation of Israel understood through God's Word that Messiah would reach out to the Gentiles, but they thought that these non Jewish people would be in a subservient position to the nation of Israel. The Mystery revealed through Christ and the Church is that, all who trust in Messiah are part of the "same body" (Ephesians 3:6). Jews and Gentiles are brought together through the life and work of Jesus Christ into one collective group of believers. We become cooperative workers as part of the same spiritual body with Jesus Christ as the head.

EXCLUSIVE OR INCLUSIVE?

Some people say that Christianity is an "exclusive" religion. They accuse Christians of not being respectful of differing religions. They contend that one religion is as good as another. But it was Jesus Himself who said, "I am the way, the truth and the life, no one comes to the Father but by Me." (John 14:6) The mystery of Messiah Jesus is that the gift of salvation He offers is indeed the only way to have a true relationship with God. It is *exclusive* in the fact that what Christ did on mankind's behalf is the only way to have forgiveness for our sins and a home in Heaven. It is *inclusive* in that it is open to anyone who is willing to believe and receive Him as Savior and Lord.

There is an amazing vision of Heaven that was given to the apostle John which he put into writing. We get a glimpse of it in Revelation 5:9-10. It shows the non-exclusive nature of God's offer of salvation to all mankind. The people giving praise to Christ are from every nationality, language, race and ethnic group. That doesn't sound too exclusive does it? Yet, all of these people groups are giving praise exclusively to Jesus Christ as their Savior because there is no other one, and no other way, which God has provided.

NEW TESTAMENT EXAMPLES

The following are some examples from other passages of the New Testament which present the exclusiveness in Jesus Christ as the only way of eternal salvation, while at the same time showing inclusiveness to all who will believe!

Simon Peter declared in his messages recorded in the book of Acts that Christ's salvation is open to all. "Whosoever shall call on the name of the Lord shall be saved." (Acts 2:21 KJV) Peter also proclaimed that though Christ is available to all who call up Him, there is no other way of salvation. "Neither is there salvation in any other: for there is no other name under heaven given among men, whereby we must be saved." (Acts 4:12 KJV).

Paul clearly affirms this same message in Romans 10:11-13 where he states that whoever believes on Jesus shall not be ashamed. He encourages us whether we are Jewish or Gentile, that "whosoever shall call upon the name of the Lord shall be saved." (Romans 10:13 KJV).

Jesus confirms with His own words, "I am the way, the truth and the life, no one comes to the Father except through me." (John 14:6 ESV) In chapter six, verses thirty-seven through forty, of John's gospel he includes other words of Jesus that carry this same idea.

John 6:37-40 "NKJV™"
37 All that the Father gives Me will come to Me, and the one who comes to Me I will by no means cast out.
38 For I have come down from heaven, not to do My own will, but the will of Him who sent Me.
39 This is the will of the Father who sent Me, that of all He has given Me I should lose nothing, but should raise it up at the last day.
40 And this is the will of Him who sent Me, that everyone who sees the Son and believes in Him may have everlasting life; and I will raise him up at the last day."

The Greek term for "sees" in verse forty is "theoreo." That word means to view attentively, to perceive with the eyes, to discern or to find out by seeing. This "seeing" involves spiritual discernment that comes from God's Holy Spirit. Once again we have an example here in Scripture that helps us understand why Paul prays for people to have "their spiritual eyes of understanding" enlightened.

Many people still perceive Jesus Christ as a mystery. They either don't believe that He is the Son of God or they haven't heard the message of the gospel or they hear but they don't really care. They don't accept what Jesus did for them on the cross of Calvary. They are faced with the dilemma of their sin and God's holiness. They are faced with the dilemma of their separation from God and how to be reconciled to Him. They are faced with the dilemma of how God could and why God would forgive their sins. It's a mystery, but God has given us enough clues through the evidence and witness of Jesus Christ to understand and reach a conclusion. It has been said that the Old Testament is Messiah concealed and the New Testament is Messiah revealed.

AN EXPLANAITION OF THE MYSTERY

Sin is universal and so are its effects on mankind. Romans 3:23 confronts us with the fact that all of us have sinned resulting in a failure of reflecting God's glory by not living the way He designed us to live. This failure separates us from God and brings death. Rescue from this failure is available through Jesus Christ. His sacrifice to God on our behalf is universal to all who will receive Him. Christ's success redeems our failure and reconciles us to God. Paul words it this way in Romans 6:23:

Romans 6:23 (KJV)
23 For the wages of sin is death; but the gift of God is eternal life through Jesus Christ our Lord.

As the one true God Man, Jesus Christ alone can be the appropriate mediator between humanity and God. Paul mentions this in his letter to Timothy.

1 Timothy 2:5 (KJV)
5 For there is one God, and one mediator between God and men, the man Christ Jesus;

Because Jesus was born of a human mother, he can represent humanity. Because God is His Father, He can bring God's power to bear on our behalf. Hebrews chapter two explains it this way:

Hebrews 2:9-10 (KJV)
9 But we see Jesus, who was made a little lower than the angels for the suffering of death, crowned with glory and honor; that he by the grace of God should taste death for every man.
10 For it became him, for whom are all things, and by whom are all things, in bringing many sons unto glory, to make the captain of their salvation perfect through sufferings.

Hebrews 2:17 (KJV)
17 Wherefore in all things it behoved him to be made like unto his brethren, that he might be a merciful and faithful high priest in things pertaining to God, to make reconciliation for the sins of the people.

Paul states in Ephesians 1:7-10 that God has revealed this wonderful mystery to us through the person and work of God's Son, Jesus Christ.

Ephesians 1:7-10 (KJV)
7 In whom we have redemption through his blood, the forgiveness of sins, according to the riches of his grace;
8 Wherein he hath abounded toward us in all wisdom and prudence;
9 Having made known unto us the mystery of his will, according to his good pleasure which he hath purposed in himself:
10 That in the dispensation of the fullness of times he might

gather together in one all things in Christ, both which are in
heaven, and which are on earth; even in him:

With any mystery there is a dilemma, clues and a
resolution. God has revealed the mystery of Messiah
in Jesus of Nazareth. He has brought the dilemma
of our sin and separation to a resolution in Christ.
He has given us many clues to investigate so that we
can understand. As the writer of Hebrews states it;

Hebrews 2:3-4 "NKJV™"
3 how shall we escape if we neglect so great a salvation,
which at the first began to be spoken by the Lord, and was
confirmed to us by those who heard Him,
4 God also bearing witness both with signs and wonders, with
various miracles, and gifts of the Holy Spirit, according to His
own will?

I pray you will more fully come to know the
love of Jesus and help reveal the mystery of Messiah
to as many others as you can.

Chapter 4
Responding To What You See

Insights from <u>Chapters Four and Five of Ephesians</u>

POTENTIAL FAITH OR KINETIC FAITH?

Potential energy is energy at rest. It is energy stored in an object by position or condition. Kinetic energy is energy in motion. Picture a rubber band in your mind that is stretched between two fingers. It has a lot of potential energy stored up in it while it is expanded. Now imagine letting go of one end and watching it fly across the room. It is releasing Kinetic energy. It is energy in motion! God wants you to put your faith in Christ into action. He doesn't want you to just keep it stored up inside yourself.

Though Paul was confined in prison because of his bold witness for Jesus, he was not discouraged and his faith was still kinetically active! He was releasing the Holy Spirit's energy at work within him as he wrote his letter to the church at Ephesus and encouraged them to be kinetic with their faith also. Paul was not letting his circumstances control his vision or his purpose in life. He was able to use his spiritual eyesight to look beyond his difficult circumstances. He could see the hope to which he was called. He could see the riches of his glorious inheritance in the saints. He was able to see the incomparably great power at work for those who believe and follow Christ.

In the first half of his letter to the church at Ephesus Paul identifies important spiritual truths we need to be aware of. In the second half of the letter he points out how we should respond to this knowledge. Paul understood that what you believe, and what you know, affects how you live. That's why Paul used the Greek words translated "therefore" or "wherefore" several times in the second half of this letter. He used these words as a signal to get our attention as he identifies each of the many ways we should respond to the knowledge of the hope, inheritance and power we have available to us in Christ. He is in essence saying, "If you understand the truths I have written about in the first half of the letter, then here are ways you should respond to God's truth with how you live." These "therefore" or "wherefore" statements appear in Ephesians chapter four and the first part of chapter five.

God's Holy Spirit within us gives us great potential, but he wants us to release that potential energy into kinetic energy. Let's look at each of these kinetic responses Paul encourages us to put in motion as we gain clearer spiritual understanding and vision.

WALK WORTH OF THE CALLING

The first "therefore" statement that Paul makes in verse one of Ephesians chapter four includes a sincere plea for us as followers of Jesus to "walk worthy of the calling" to which Christ has given us.

Of course we know to walk involves action and motion that moves us in a specific direction. So to walk worthy of the calling which you have received in Christ Jesus means to go in the direction He wants you to travel in life. It means to begin living like Jesus wants you to live. God has given us an extraordinary calling in Christ. How we respond makes all the difference! We need to learn to live with His hope, according to His riches of grace, and by His power! The power that God has placed in your life through the indwelling of His Holy Spirit needs to be released through you. When this power is combined with other believers through the community and fellowship of the church, it becomes mighty and effective to the rest of the world.

Paul describes in the first six verses the attitude we should have as we live out our faith in Christ.

Ephesians 4:1-6 "NKJV™"
1 I, therefore, the prisoner of the Lord, beseech you to walk worthy of the calling with which you were called,
2 with all lowliness and gentleness, with longsuffering, bearing with one another in love,
3 endeavoring to keep the unity of the Spirit in the bond of peace.
4 There is one body and one Spirit, just as you were called in one hope of your calling;
5 one Lord, one faith, one baptism;
6 one God and Father of all, who is above all, and through all, and in you all.

Look closely at verse three of Ephesians chapter four. Spiritual unity is not something we have to manufacture or coerce. The oneness of believers in Christ is already a spiritual reality. Our responsibility is to guard, protect, and preserve that unity. That's what "endeavoring to keep the unity" means in verse three. Emphasis is not on a certain group or denomination but on the founder of our faith, Jesus Christ. The spiritual unity of a home, a ministry team, a small group, or a church is the responsibility of each person involved, and the job never ends! This unity is based on the truth and person of Jesus Christ in response to God's gift of grace.

USE YOUR SPIRITUAL GIFTS AND ABILITIES TO STRENGTHEN HIS CHURCH

The second response we should have as we come to understand the power and abilities that Christ has enabled us with, is to put those abilities to use in helping His church grow by serving.

Ephesians 4:7-16 (KJV)
7 But <u>unto every one of us is given grace according to the measure of the gift of Christ</u>.
8 **Wherefore** he saith, When he ascended up on high, he led captivity captive, and gave gifts unto men.
9 (Now that he ascended, what is it but that he also descended first into the lower parts of the earth?
10 He that descended is the same also that ascended up far above all heavens, that he might fill all things.)

11 And he gave some, apostles; and some, prophets; and some, evangelists; and some, pastors and teachers;
12 For the perfecting of the saints, for the work of the ministry, for the edifying of the body of Christ:
13 Till we all come in the unity of the faith, and of the knowledge of the Son of God, unto a perfect man, unto the measure of the stature of the fulness of Christ:
14 That we henceforth be no more children, tossed to and fro, and carried about with every wind of doctrine, by the sleight of men, and cunning craftiness, whereby they lie in wait to deceive;
15 But speaking the truth in love, may grow up into him in all things, which is the head, even Christ:
16 From whom the whole body fitly joined together and compacted by that which every joint supplieth, according to the effectual working in the measure of every part, maketh increase of the body unto the edifying of itself in love.

A spiritual gift is a Holy Spirit given ability to serve in such a way that Christ is glorified and His church is edified. Every person in the church is to contribute to the overall health, work, and growth of the church. The spiritual gifts and service mentioned in verse eleven are not all inclusive. Other spiritual gifts that bless humanity and help grow the church are identified in 1 Corinthians chapter twelve, Romans chapter twelve, as well as 1 Peter chapter four. Just a few examples of these abilities are teaching, administration, compassion, hospitality, giving and leading.

If you want to continue to develop your spiritual eyesight, take some time to read and study those passages. Get to know what these gifts are and how they operate. As you become aware of what gifts you may have, begin to put them into practice along with other people in the church. Use your gifts and abilities to serve and help others. The apostle Peter specifically encourages us to do this.

1 Peter 4:10 (KJV)
10 As every man hath received the gift, even so minister the same one to another, as good stewards of the manifold grace of God.

By His grace God gives at least one spiritual gift to each person who trusts fully in Christ. These gifts or abilities are to be used to help His church be healthy and grow. As we practice using these gifts, we continue to help our spiritual eyesight develop and become more aware of God's calling, hope, riches and power working in and through us.

DON'T LIVE LIKE PEOPLE WHO ARE SPIRITUALLY DEAD AND MISLED

Ephesians 4:17-24 (KJV)
17 This I say **therefore**, and testify in the Lord, that ye henceforth walk not as other Gentiles walk, in the vanity of their mind,

18 Having the understanding darkened, being alienated from the life of God through the ignorance that is in them, because of the blindness of their heart:
19 Who being past feeling have given themselves over unto lasciviousness, to work all uncleanness with greediness.
20 But ye have not so learned Christ;
21 If so be that ye have heard him, and have been taught by him, as the truth is in Jesus:
22 That ye put off concerning the former conversation the old man, which is corrupt according to the deceitful lusts;
23 And be renewed in the spirit of your mind;
24 And that ye put on the new man, which after God is created in righteousness and true holiness.

We need to put our faith into motion by serving the Lord and helping others. We also need to put our faith into motion by working against ungodly behavior. Paul points out in verse eighteen that there are many people who are "alienated" from the spiritual life of God because of spiritual blindness in their heart. They use their time and energy pursuing self seeking pleasure instead of a relationship with God. In this sense they are spiritually dead. That's why Jesus taught that unless we are "born again" we cannot see the Kingdom of God, (John 3:3). We need to be given a spiritual birth through the presence of God's Holy Spirit regenerating our spirit as we believe and receive Jesus as our Savior.

People who are spiritually dead are misled. Their spiritual eyes of understanding are blinded to the truth of God in Christ. They follow the futility of their own thinking, rather than the truth of God's Word. This doesn't mean they are unintelligent. Many spiritually dead people are extremely intelligent, but their intelligence is still insufficient and incomplete in relationship to God. Paul refers to it as the "futility of their minds" in reference to spiritual things. This leads them to think that if God exists, they can't know Him, or that they need to figure God out on their own. Some just create their own version of the kind of god they want. Still others are convinced He doesn't exist at all. Many who are spiritually dead seek to fill the void in their life through human achievements, accolades, over indulgence, seeking constant pleasure, power, money, various philosophical viewpoints and a host of other pursuits.

We are cautioned to remember that as Christians, our minds have not only been changed, but our citizenship has been changed. When baseball players are traded from one team to another, they put on a new uniform that represents the team they are now playing for. They no longer wear the uniform of the team for which they used to play. They do their best to help their new team win. Paul draws an analogy for us as Christians of changing clothes. We are to put on the new uniform so to speak, of a new demeanor and lifestyle. We are to identify ourselves with Christ by conducting ourselves according to His character living in and through us. We are not part of the old team of the sinful world, but we have been purchased by the blood of Christ and chosen by Him to be on His team and in His Kingdom! We need to live by His principles. In order to continue to live by this new character that Christ has put within us, we must not give the devil a place in our lives to gain influence once again. That brings us to a fourth kinetic motion of our faith indicated by another "therefore" which Paul uses.

DON'T GIVE THE DEVIL A PLACE

There are many ways we can knowingly or unsuspectingly allow the devil to gain influence in our lives. Paul points out the importance of staying on guard as you put your faith into action.

Ephesians 4:25-32 (KJV)
25 <u>Wherefore</u> putting away lying, speak every man truth with his neighbour: for we are members one of another.
26 Be ye angry, and sin not: let not the sun go down upon your wrath:
27 **Neither give place to the devil.**
28 Let him that stole steal no more: but rather let him labour, working with his hands the thing which is good, that he may have to give to him that needeth.

29 Let no corrupt communication proceed out of your mouth, but that which is good to the use of edifying, that it may minister grace unto the hearers.
30 And grieve not the holy Spirit of God, whereby ye are sealed unto the day of redemption.
31 Let all bitterness, and wrath, and anger, and clamour, and evil speaking, be put away from you, with all malice:
32 And be ye kind one to another, tenderhearted, forgiving one another, even as God for Christ's sake hath forgiven you.

What are ways followers of Christ still "give place to the devil" in their lives? Unforgiveness, pent up anger and unfit speech such as gossip are a few examples Paul cites in verses twenty-five through thirty-one. God's Spirit in us is grieved and the devil gains a place in us when we let bitterness, uncontrolled anger and evil speaking go unchecked in our lives.

Social networking through electronic media is extremely popular today. We can connect with people we want to stay in touch with, even when we are separated geographically by great distances. One of the ways we connect with others is through a Myspace or Facebook page on the internet. In order to connect with people this way you have to allow them access as a friend to your webpage on that account. Considering Paul's warning not to give the devil a place in your life think of it this way; Don't give the Devil a Myspace place in your life. Don't give the Devil access to the Facebook page of your life anymore. "Unfriend" him!

Don't give the Devil a presence or place of influence to work and represent himself in your mind and heart. Don't let him in on your spiritual network. We allow Satan to gain a place in our mind and heart when we get involved in activities that are opposed to God's will for our lives. When we play around with temptations that the devil brings our way or exposes us to. Where Satan gets a finger hold, he will try to get a foothold, and he won't be satisfied until he moves in and establishes a stronghold in your life. So don't open the door to give him a place to begin with!

IMITATE JESUS CHRIST

Paul continues his "therefore" statements about the ways we should respond to the knowledge of Christ we are gaining.

Ephesians 5:1-5 "NKJV™"
1 <u>Therefore</u> be imitators of God as dear children.
2 And walk in love, as Christ also has loved us and given Himself for us, an offering and a sacrifice to God for a sweet-smelling aroma.
3 But fornication and all uncleanness or covetousness, let it not even be named among you, as is fitting for saints;
4 neither filthiness, nor foolish talking, nor coarse jesting, which are not fitting, but rather giving of thanks.
5 For this you know, that no fornicator, unclean person, nor

covetous man, who is an idolater, has any inheritance in the kingdom of Christ and God.

Through the life of Jesus Christ, God showed us how He intended humanity to live. He demonstrated great character, humility, knowledge, love, compassion, service and a healthy relationship with God and others. He wants us to imitate Him. We need the indwelling and filling of His Holy Spirit to do this. We receive the indwelling of His Spirit when we open our hearts and invite Christ into our lives as Savior. As we yield ourselves to His Spirit work within us He begins to change us. This process is a continual exercise of faith. He begins to give us new healthy desires that battle against the desires of our sin nature such as sexual immorality, dishonesty, greed, and selfishness. God has taught us that these characteristics have no place in His Kingdom. We must adjust to His Kingdom, not expect His Kingdom to adjust to us. God is giving us the opportunity now to prepare for His Kingdom which is composed of characteristics that are much better for us and for His glory. This preparation is not about us trying to be good enough to get there. Christ has already accomplished that for us. It is about us responding to His grace. It is about us cooperating with the work His Holy Spirit is doing in us to prepare us for the riches of His inheritance in eternity.

SOME THINGS TO THINK ABOUT

A few good questions for you to ask yourself are, "Who am I imitating with my life? Who am I patterning my lifestyle after? Who is my role model? In what ways am I cooperating with God's Word and the Holy Spirit's work in my life? In what ways am I resisting?"

WALK AS CHILDREN OF LIGHT

Paul continues by issuing a warning to be on guard against being enticed by the lure of corrupt or evil worldly desires and temporary pleasures that have destructive consequences.

Ephesians 5:6-13 "NKJV™"
6 Let no one deceive you with empty words, for because of these things the wrath of God comes upon the sons of disobedience.
7 <u>Therefore</u> do not be partakers with them.
8 For you were once darkness, but now you are light in the Lord. Walk as children of light
9 (for the fruit of the Spirit is in all goodness, righteousness, and truth),
10 finding out what is acceptable to the Lord.
11 And have no fellowship with the unfruitful works of darkness, but rather expose them
12 For it is shameful even to speak of those things which are done by them in secret.
13 But all things that are exposed are made manifest by the light, for whatever makes manifest is light.

To "walk as children of light" means to live according to the principles of God's Word. It means to cooperate with the power of Christ's Holy Spirit living within you in such a way that others can see Christ through you. It means to use discipline and self control in your conduct. It means instead of trying to excuse sinful tendencies in your life, that you admit they are sinful and ask God to help you. (Look again at Ephesians 5:8-9.)

Throughout the Bible God's Word is described as light. (A few examples of this are found in Psalm 119:105, John 1:1-14, John 8:12 and 1 John 1:1-7). To "walk as children of light" means to live in agreement with what God's Word instructs us. Instead of fighting against what He teaches us, we allow His Word to expose our sins and the errors in our thinking and we abide by His wisdom. That's what Paul is referring to in verse ten when he writes "finding out what is acceptable to the Lord."

Paul instructs us that as we begin to understand by the light of God's Word what is the hope, riches and power we have available to us through Jesus Christ, we begin to live by new standards. That's what he means when he writes in verse eight, "For you were once darkness, but now you are light in the Lord. Walk as children of light." Instead of rationalizing our sinful behaviors and making excuses to continue in them, we admit them to Christ. We let the piercing light of God's Word expose in us the things that are not acceptable to Him and we surrender them over to Him rather than clinging to them.

If you have traveled on public airlines recently you understand what it's like to go through airport security. You have to be willing to surrender your luggage to special x-ray imaging equipment where everything inside can be seen. You have to submit yourself to a scan and even a search to make sure there is nothing inappropriate or harmful to others being brought along with you on the trip. To walk as children of light means that we continually allow the light of God's Word and His Holy Spirit to reveal in us any wrong attitude, belief or conduct that is not appropriate for His Kingdom, so we can surrender it over to Him!

OPEN YOUR EYES!

If we are going to put our faith into action we must constantly be on the lookout for opportunities to be a positive witness for Christ in the world. We need to be aware that people are watching our lifestyle to see if it lines up with what we say we believe. We need to make the most of the opportunities each day that God gives us as we interact with family, friends, neighbors, co-workers and others in the church. Paul points this out in verses fourteen through sixteen of Ephesians chapter five.

Ephesians 5:14-16 "NKJV™"
14 <u>Therefore</u> He says: "Awake, you who sleep, Arise from the dead, And Christ will give you light."
15 See then that you walk circumspectly, not as fools but as wise,
16 redeeming the time, because the days are evil.

There are a lot of people who are spiritually sleep walking. They go through life oblivious of the spiritual dynamics at work in their midst. Paul warns us to wake up. We need to become aware of what's happening around us in the spiritual realm and respond accordingly. That's what "walk circumspectly" means in verse fifteen. This topic is covered more specifically in chapter six of this book.

Paul uses the phrase "redeeming the time" in verse sixteen. That means to make the most of the time we have left for doing good instead of evil. We need to help shine the light of the good news of God's grace through Jesus Christ to others. We need to help them see the hope, riches and power they can have available to them through faith in Him. We can't afford to sleep walk through the time we have left here on earth as we wait to go to Heaven. If you are not kinetically putting your faith into action, it's time for you to wake up and get in motion.

What have you wanted to do for His Kingdom or for His church, but thought that you were not qualified? Is there something you have been sensing that the Lord wants you to do to help someone else, but you have been reluctant to follow through? Pray and search Scriptures to make sure that what you are sensing is in agreement with the principles His Word teaches. If the Bible and other mature Christ followers confirm what you are sensing, then step out in faith and do it. Release the potential energy of your faith and use the gifts that God has given you to help others come to know Him! That brings us to the final "therefore" in chapter five that Paul uses to identify the responses we should put into action as a result of our growing faith and knowledge in Christ.

UNDERSTAND WHAT THE WILL OF THE LORD IS AND DO IT

Paul sums up his list of action points with a broad statement that indicates an ongoing process of learning and doing.

Ephesians 5:17-21 "NKJV™"
17 Therefore do not be unwise, but understand what the will of the Lord is.

18 And do not be drunk with wine, in which is dissipation; but
be filled with the Spirit,
19 speaking to one another in psalms and hymns and spiritual
songs, singing and making melody in your heart to the Lord,
20 giving thanks always for all things to God the Father in the
name of our Lord Jesus Christ,
21 submitting to one another in the fear of God.

We discover the will of God as He illumines our
mind through reading His word, praying,
worshipping God and fellowshipping with other
believers. We each need to get to know other
followers of Christ and let them get to know us.
Paul describes the importance of making the most of
the life and time God gives us. He uses a play on
words to make the point that it is better to be filled
with the effects of God's Holy Spirit in our lives than
to be filled with the effects of wine which leads to
drunkenness.

From ancient times man discovered ways of
getting intoxicated through ingesting substances from
plants or drink. Wine was an important product in
Biblical times. Drinking wine in moderation was not
a sin, but intoxication was strongly spoken against.
You will find examples of problems associated with
drunkenness throughout the Old Testament. You
will also find many examples of problems associated
with intoxication in the news today each week. It is
not a new problem. The unchanging truth is that
drunkenness leads to all kinds of reckless behavior,

but being empowered and filled with God's Holy Spirit leads to all kinds of beneficial behavior. Being filled with the awareness and presence of Christ's Spirit in your life gives you a sense of true joy that lasts a lot longer than an alcoholic buzz or a drug high.

Paul continues his comparison of partying with wine and partying in the Spirit of God by mentioning singing, gladness and thanksgiving. Singing and making music helps us connect our thoughts and emotions with each other. It is a powerful medium. It helps us share in our sense of sorrows or joy together. As followers of Christ, music is a great way to connect with others who are on the journey with us. It is a great way to learn scripture and remember principles and promises of God. If you can't sing, you can still have a melody in your heart. You can remember the melodies and sing the songs in your mind as you think about the words which help you express and strengthen your faith.

Paul mentions three types of musical songs. The Greek word Paul uses in verse nineteen that is translated into English as "psalms" actually means a striking of chords on a musical instrument in playing a religious song. The Greek word translated as "hymns" in that same verse means a sacred song of praise to God. The third Greek term "spiritual" songs implies songs that come from the soul of man but are divinely inspired from God's Spirit. They come from a person who is filled and governed by the Spirit of God. We see these three types of music and songs in the church today through traditional music, hymns, contemporary praise songs and choruses.

Note that in this passage Paul does not say one style of musical song is better than the other. Churches who become divided or divisive over the issue of music styles in the church are allowing the devil to disrupt the unity that we are intended to work together to keep. (See Ephesians 4:2-3) There can be a place for each musical song style as God's Holy Spirit leads and gives discernment.

After Paul addresses the issue of music he makes an important transition statement next in Ephesians 5:21 about the heart we should have for cooperation amongst each other. As people who are seeking to understand and follow Christ's will for our lives, Paul says we are to be "submitting to one another in the fear of God". This emphasizes our interdependence as we follow the leading of Christ's Spirit working among us, in us, and through us, with the various gifts and abilities He gives us to use. We are to work together in the various roles and assignments He has given us. The Greek word for "submitting" that is used in this verse means "a voluntary attitude of giving in, cooperating, assuming responsibility, and carrying a burden." [3] When each person voluntarily cooperates for the good of the whole and for the glory of Christ, we all benefit and are blessed. This same attitude needs to be exemplified in our family relationships. Paul addresses that topic next in his letter which is the focus of chapter five of this book.

Are you beginning to get the picture? Is your spiritual eyesight beginning to come into clearer focus? When you truly begin to have your spiritual eyes of understanding enlightened, when you begin to properly understand the hope of your calling, the glorious riches of your inheritance in the saints, and the incomparably great power that God works toward you as you believe, it will impact every area of our life. It will change your worldview and how you live.

Potential energy is energy at rest. Kinetic energy is energy in motion. As God's Holy Spirit enters your life and stretches you by His power with new potential for His Kingdom, put it in motion to bless others. Release it for God's glory!

---

[3] Strong, James: *The Exhaustive Concordance of the Bible : Showing Every Word of the Test of the Common English Version of the Canonical Books, and Every Occurence of Each Word in Regular Order*. electronic ed. Ontario : Woodside Bible Fellowship., 1996, S. H0

Chapter 5
Realizing God's Plan For Family

Insights from <u>chapters five and six of Ephesians</u>

MARRIAGE OR MELEE ?

I heard an interesting story about a wedding reception at a church in a small community. After the wedding took place in the sanctuary, the happy newlyweds made their way to the dining hall of the church where the reception was held. They toasted each other, cut the cake, and had their pictures taken together at the table like many couples do.

They were so wrapped up in their celebration, that they didn't notice one of the many framed Bible verses that decorated the walls of the church in the area that was directly behind where the wedding cake table was located. Most of the Bible verses referred to God's love and care, but it just so happened that the Bible verse on the wall where they had their pictures taken displayed a quote from Luke chapter three verse seven which proclaims, "Flee from the wrath to come!"

Unfortunately this phrase becomes prophetic in many marriages. More often than not, we see examples of family relationships that are torn with strife, discontent, disappointment and unfaithfulness. God designed marriage to be a loyal life-time union between a man and a woman. It is out of that union that the basic family unit of society is formed and stabilized. But like everything else that has been affected by the sin nature of mankind in the world, so too, has the image of marriage been marred.

It is troubling to see that God's design for marriage has become so ignored and disfigured in our culture that there is a growing contingent of people who are trying to redefine marriage as they think best. These attempts at happiness are ultimately doomed to failure, because the problem isn't the design of marriage which God set forth. The problem is our stubborn human nature that is reluctant to cooperate with God's design. Jesus pointed this fact out one day when he was asked a question by some religious leaders about "no fault divorce" which was prevalent at that time. This question is recorded in Matthew 19:3.

Matthew 19:3-8 "NKJV™"
3 The Pharisees also came to Him, testing Him, and saying to Him, "Is it lawful for a man to divorce his wife for just any reason?"
4 And He answered and said to them, "Have you not read that He who made them at the beginning 'made them male and female,'
5 and said, 'For this reason a man shall leave his father and mother and be joined to his wife, and the two shall become one flesh' ?
6 So then, they are no longer two but one flesh. Therefore what God has joined together, let not man separate."
7 They said to Him, "Why then did Moses command to give a certificate of divorce, and to put her away?"
8 He said to them, "Moses, because of the hardness of your hearts, permitted you to divorce your wives, but from the beginning it was not so.

In giving his answer to the Pharisees, Jesus referred to the creation account recorded in the book of Genesis. He did this to remind them that God designed marriage to be a mutually caring relationship for a life-time. He answered their question by saying the heart of the problem was not with God's design or with the law of Moses, but with people. In our sinful condition we often let our hearts become self centered and unfaithful. Whether it is one person misbehaving in the relationship or both, divorce ultimately is caused by someone's hard-heartedness. The result is always emotional pain and heartache inflicted on each other which God never intended.

As we read the Genesis account that Jesus referred to, we see that God made man and woman in His image. In Genesis 2:18-24 we learn that God designed the relationship between Adam and Eve to be one of mutual caring, sharing and wholeness. As the progenitors of the human race, they were to form the basis of the family unit with mutual commitment and support. This was to be the model for marriage.

God created Adam from the dust of the ground and breathed into his nostrils the breath of life. This imagery shows the close intimate relationship that God desires to have with humanity. After God created Adam, He performed the first surgery in recorded history. He put Adam to sleep, removed one of Adam's ribs and used it as the basis to form woman. By this Adam would know that Eve was specially made as a companion for him. Likewise God did this so that Eve would know that she shared a part of Adam that nothing else in creation could. She was to have a special relationship with him because he was a part of her, and she was made from him. Together they were to bear offspring and enjoy life as a family unit with God's blessing and presence. This is God's design for marriage as it should be. When we look at the creation description of Adam and Eve with spiritual eyes of understanding we can see how God was demonstrating His intent for this special relationship.

In God's awesome plan, He brought woman into the world through man, and then gave woman the ability to conceive and bear children so that through her, man could come into the world. This was to be the basic family unit. One man, one woman, bound together for life in commitment to each other and harmony with God as they bore children and raised them to adulthood.

Matthew Henry has been attributed with the following quote. "Eve was not made by God out of the head to rule over Adam, nor out of his feet to be trampled upon by him, but out of his side to be equal with him, and near his heart to be loved."

Marriage is to be a loving, caring relationship where both husband and wife honor and respect each other, and live in relationship with God.

Sad to say, we all know that most marriages are not like this. Though sin in the world and disobedience to God's blueprint for marriage has resulted in many broken families, this design is not an unachievable goal. That is why God's Spirit led Paul to remind the followers of Christ at Ephesus about the importance of this sacred relationship.

TWO SHALL BECOME ONE

In his letter to the Ephesians, as Paul addresses the issue of marriage, he followed the example of Jesus by referring to Genesis to get the proper foundation and framework for understanding God's design. Paul describes it in Ephesians 5:31-33.

Ephesians 5:31-33 "NKJV™"
31 "For this reason a man shall leave his father and mother and be joined to his wife, and the two shall become one flesh."
32 This is a great mystery, but I speak concerning Christ and the church.
33 Nevertheless let each one of you in particular so love his own wife as himself, and let the wife see that she respects her husband.

The phrase "the two shall become one flesh" is an interesting expression. We understand it to metaphorically describe intimacy in the marriage relationship. Paul takes it further by saying God designed the marriage union ultimately to be an object lesson to the world of the relationship between Jesus Christ and His church.

As you think of the phrase, "For this reason a man shall leave his father and mother and be joined to his wife," think about the fact that Christ left His home in Heaven to enter into this world and gave His life sacrificially for us so we could be joined with Him. In so doing, we are reconciled to God Himself through the love initiated on His behalf toward us in Christ. Now look at the phrase, "and the two shall become one flesh." Paul has already described earlier in his letter to the Ephesians the mystery of Messiah and how we are all united into His "one body" of believers through faith in Christ and the indwelling of His Holy Spirit in our lives. Paul is implying that when marriage works the way God designed it to work, it is a beautiful picture of the loyalty, love, responsibility and choice that Jesus Christ has made toward mankind, and the proper way we should respond to the loving choice that He has made.

God designed marriage for stability, loyalty and mutual support as children are brought into the world and raised to adulthood. God does not want husband and wife to be in struggles for superiority in the relationship, but working cooperatively in service to each other.

In chapter four and continuing in chapter five of his letter, Paul has gone to great lengths to picture the unity, cooperation, and shared responsibility that each person in the church should work toward for the overall good and growth of the church. He sums it up in Ephesians 5:21 by saying, "Submit to one another out of reverence for Christ." This carries over to help us understand what he now explains as God's special relationship roles in the family. He details it in Ephesians 5:22-29.

Ephesians 5:22 "NKJV™"
22 Wives, submit to your own husbands, as to the Lord.
23 For the husband is head of the wife, as also Christ is head of the church; and He is the Savior of the body.
24 Therefore, just as the church is subject to Christ, so let the wives be to their own husbands in everything.
25 Husbands, love your wives, just as Christ also loved the church and gave Himself for her,
26 that He might sanctify and cleanse her with the washing of water by the word,
27 that He might present her to Himself a glorious church, not having spot or wrinkle or any such thing, but that she should be holy and without blemish.
28 So husbands ought to love their own wives as their own bodies; he who loves his wife loves himself.
29 For no one ever hated his own flesh, but nourishes and cherishes it, just as the Lord does the church.
30 For we are members of His body, of His flesh and of His bones.

SHARED RESPECT - SHARED RESPONSIBILITY

In light of this knowledge, healthy marriage and family relationships must consist of two mutual elements that reflect true love. Those mutual elements are shared respect and shared responsibility. These essentials are to be given sacrificially by both husband and wife to each other, for the benefit of each other. It doesn't work when one person is doing most of the giving and the other is doing most of the taking.

In Paul's time, many in the culture saw women as inferior beings to the dominant male. The wife was not equal to her husband as a person, or in any other way. His needs and concerns dominated the household, and the wife existed to fulfill those needs and to serve him. This is *not* how God designed marriage to work. There are cultures and individuals in the world today who still hold to that viewpoint. Over the past several decades as a reaction to that improper view of marriage, extremists of the feminist movement have gone so far as to try and elevate women to a status above men. This is not healthy or realistic either.

In contrast to these views, God's perspective on the marriage relationship shows that men and women are seen as persons of equal worth and value in his sight, with different roles. In God's structure of marriage and family, men are given the role of head of the family. But their headship is modeled on the way Christ loved the church, not on human systems of authority. This headship focuses attention and responsibility of the one who is in leadership to care for and coordinate the ones who are under his realm of responsibility. In God's order of creating humanity in His image, He made man first, and then out of the man, He made woman. Remember this was not a demeaning act, but a beautiful picture of God creating intimacy between man and woman. God said it was not good for man to be alone. Woman is God's special creation to acknowledge man's need from a human perspective. Man and woman fulfill and complete each other under God's design. God also created woman in this manner to show the man's obligation to cherish and care for his wife, and the wife's obligation to be a companion and help for her husband. Any other attempt to redefine marriage partners or roles is doomed to failure and lack of fulfillment.

Ephesians 5:27 portrays Christ as giving Himself up for the church "to present her to Himself as a radiant church, without stain or wrinkle or any other blemish, but holy and blameless." In the same way, Christian husbands are to nurture their wives, seeking always to help the wife grow as a person and as a Christian. Instead of demanding that she sacrifice for him, he is willing to make sacrifices for her well being! Instead of keeping her down, he seeks to lift her up. In response to this kind of loving leadership, the wife should respond with cooperation and respect to the husband who lifts her up and holds her beside him. These are not power struggles, but roles that give us different opportunities to serve each other. The model here is not competition, but cooperation. Not superiority, but service to each other. Husbands and wives must respect and value each other.

There are many resources available today to help couples strengthen their marriages. Some good books which have stood the test of time and are still available today are His Needs, Her Needs by Willard F. Harley Jr., Love and Respect by Dr. Everson Eggerichs, and The Five Love Languages by Gary Chapman. Though these books are written from a modern perspective and are not necessarily considered religious books, they certainly reflect the basic principles of God's design for marriage that Paul defines toward the end of Ephesians chapter five.

As our spiritual eyesight continues to develop we also begin to see more clearly God's design for family relationships when it comes to proper parent/child relationships. Paul describes it in foundational form with the simplest of wording in Ephesians 6:1-4.

Ephesians 6:1-4 (KJV)
1 Children, obey your parents in the Lord: for this is right.
2 Honour thy father and mother; (which is the first commandment with promise;)
3 That it may be well with thee, and thou mayest live long on the earth.
4 And, ye fathers, provoke not your children to wrath: but bring them up in the nurture and admonition of the Lord.

It's interesting to note that Paul points out to fathers the importance of not treating their children in an overly harsh manner. It is necessary to discipline children. It is a vital part of the learning process. There are many passages in the Bible that highlight the importance of disciplining our children and the disastrous results for those who don't. God's design for parenting has never been for parents to be abusive to children in their discipline.

Perhaps some of you reading this now have painful memories of abuse you suffered in some way from one or both of your parents at some point as you were growing up. If so, you understand the feelings of helplessness, frustration and even anger that can well up in a person who has experienced abuse. You can probably especially relate to what Paul means in verse four when he refers to being provoked to wrath. If you had a parent who claimed to be a follower of Christ, but who was abusive to you in some way, you need to understand that they were allowing their sin nature

82

to control them at that point. They were not practicing what Christ's Word teaches.

On the other hand, God does not want parents to give in to every demand of their children. This results in children who grow to adulthood with a sense of entitlement and selfishness. With a bit of humor, Edward VIII, Duke of Windsor (1894-1972) had this to say about our society after he visited America: "The thing that impresses me most about North America is the way parents obey their children." Sad to say, but I have seen many examples of this. In an attempt to avoid being overly harsh, many parents are overly easy on their kids. They don't want to upset their children or make them unhappy so they give in to their immature complaints, whims or tantrums, just to quiet them down. Other parents fail to discipline their children for fear that their children will not like them anymore. The Bible speaks the truth in Hebrews chapter twelve as it describes that though no discipline is pleasant to go through at the time, it later yields the peaceable fruit of righteousness to those who have been trained by it. When our fathers discipline us rightly, we respect them instead of despising them. Children tend to despise parents who don't care enough to discipline them.

The late Dr Alberta Siegel who was a professor of psychology at Stanford University wrote the following often cited quote in the Stanford Observer:

"Twenty years is all we have to accomplish the task of civilizing the infants who are born into our midst each year. These savages know nothing of our language, our culture, our religion, our values, or our customs of interpersonal relations. The infant is totally ignorant about communism, fascism, democracy, civil liberties, rights of the minority as contrasted with the prerogatives of the majority, respect, decency, honesty, customs, conventions, and manners. The barbarian must be tamed if civilization is to survive."[4]

Though this depiction of children may seem overly brazen, the premise is correct. Children need to be properly educated and disciplined. They, like us, have been born with a sin nature that needs to be addressed. God expects parents to properly discipline, teach and train their children. God also expects children to honor and obey their parents. It is part of learning to respect God's authority over our lives.

---

[4] Stanford Observer, October 1973, p. 4, quoted in Kerux illustration #2305

CONTRIBUTORS OR CONSUMERS ?

Most parents are pretty good about teaching their children how to feed themselves, how to dress themselves and how to be potty trained, but parenting of course is much more than this. As parents it's our job to raise responsible adults, not selfish consumers. As parents who are followers of Christ it is also our responsibility to lovingly guide our children into a saving and productive knowledge of God's Word and faith in Jesus Christ. This is done best by consistently modeling Christ-like character in our homes. As we allow Christ's Spirit to shape and mold us, our children will see that God's Word is more than just talk, it is action. Sacrifice, commitment, and service are principles that need to be demonstrated in the home beginning with the parents, and taught through practice among the children.

The same two mutual elements of shared respect and shared responsibility which reflect true love among husband and wife must be demonstrated and taught among the children as well. Siblings need to be taught shared respect for each other and shared responsibility of helping in the home. Children and parents need to share proper levels of respect and responsibility as everyone involved works for the good of the family unit. This is the way God designed families to work, and it's the way they work best.

Many think this picture of marriage is an unachievable ideal, but it is not. Satan has managed to distort and blur our image of what marriage is supposed to be. That is why we must personally ask for God's Spirit to empower and help us do our part in upholding God's vision and design for marriage that He created. Examples of families where husbands and wives have stayed together, properly loved, disciplined and taught their children, and whose children have grown up to be productive responsible adults are still celebrated in every culture. This ought to tell us something about the foundational design God has intended for society.

After helping us see God's intent and design for healthy family relationships, Paul goes on in his letter and addresses other relationships that involve authority and submission. Paul takes on the issue of relationships between slaves and masters in verses five through nine of Ephesians chapter six.

Thankfully, the issue of slavery has been done away with as an acceptable practice in our culture, but during the time that Paul wrote this letter it was still widely in use. As you read this passage you will notice that Paul is not condoning slavery. His intent was to help both those who were slaves and slave owners to see through spiritual eyes how they should respond to each other in this cultural situation that they were in.

We can apply the same basic principles Paul taught in this passage concerning relationships between slaves and masters to our modern day employee and employer relationships. Some of you may work for an employer in a situation where you feel like there is no difference! To help apply this passage to our current working relationships today, when you see the word "slave" think of "employee" and when you see the word "master" think of the word "manager" or "employer" or "boss."

Ephesians 6:5-9 (ESV)
5 Slaves, obey your earthly masters with fear and trembling, with a sincere heart, as you would Christ,
6 not by the way of eye-service, as people-pleasers, but as servants of Christ, doing the will of God from the heart,
7 rendering service with a good will as to the Lord and not to man,
8 knowing that whatever good anyone does, this he will receive back from the Lord, whether he is a slave or free.
9 Masters, do the same to them, and stop your threatening, knowing that he who is both their Master and yours is in heaven, and that there is no partiality with him.

As we begin to see all of our relationships in life through spiritual eyes of understanding, we begin to realize that each one of us is important to God, no matter what our position in life, and so is everyone else! God wants us to see each person's value and purpose in life apart from their role or position. The employee is just as important to God as the employer, the child as the parent, the woman as the man. The Christian view of authority and submission shifts the focus completely from power, to service. We are reminded in Galatians 5:13 "through love, serve one another" and in Ephesians 5:21 "submit to one another out of reverence for Christ."

Paul wants to help us realize that our place in society is immaterial to the oneness that God designed to exist in His church. As Christians we are to serve one another equally and be a blessing to the world for Christ's glory. In Christ, slave and master are one. They are equal. In Christ male and female are equal. In Christ Jew and Gentile are equal. How silly of us then to define each other in the church by race or social status and feel the alienation which that creates. If you are an employer, you serve your employees by treating them with fairness and respect. If you are an employee, you serve your employer with wholehearted loyalty. If you are a husband you serve your wife in order to build her up and help her reach her full potential. If you are a wife, you support your husband with respect, appreciation, and devotion. As a child you are to do what your parents ask you in order to learn responsibility and to help you and your family grow.

As parents you are to treat your children appropriately and responsibly.

It is very freeing to realize that your worth and value as a person rests on who you are in Christ, and that your position in the world simply defines your opportunities to serve. Shared respect and shared responsibility are two elements that are vital to any healthy relationship. Are you modeling them in your home, on your job, and in the church?

SOME THINGS TO THINK ABOUT

Who comes to mind when you think about couples who have demonstrated a healthy marriage relationship? What characteristics did they display in their marriage that stand out most in your mind? If you are married, what characteristics do you need to work on in your marriage? If you are not married, what characteristics are most important to you in finding a mate to marry? Are there any families that you have observed who have done a good job of parenting? How did they display those good skills? How are their children doing now?

Chapter 6

Preparing For Spiritual Warfare

Insights from chapter six of Ephesians

We are at war. It is much broader and deeper than the war in Afghanistan, Libya, Iraq or wherever else in the world our troops may be called to fight. This war involves our families, our friends, our co-workers, our nation, and indeed all inhabitants of the earth. This war is so insidious that many people don't even recognize or acknowledge it. They know something isn't right, but they can't put their finger on it.

With spiritual eyesight, the apostle Paul points directly at the problem to help us see it. In Ephesians chapter six verse twelve he explains that this struggle is not against "flesh and blood" but it is a spiritual warfare. A battle against wickedness, spiritual darkness and the power of Satan at work through various means in the world today.

One of the tactics that the devil uses is camouflage. He knows his work will not be as effective if he is discovered. He loves to disguise himself in the form of something that looks desirable. His weapons are temptation, deceit, fear, intimidation, discouragement, and illusion just to name a few. He loves to lure us into behaviors that are enjoyable for awhile, but end up having dire consequences for our lives. He loves to get us fighting against each other and discouraged against God. His goal is to thwart God's plan for mankind. He knows he can't defeat God, so he goes after mankind as God's prized possession. The Bible teaches us that human beings are the crown of God's creation. In all of creation only humanity is spoken of in the Bible as being made "in God's image."

Satan succeeded in luring Adam and Eve away from God by enticing them to disobey God's most simple command of trust and obedience in the very beginning. The rest of humanity has followed that direction ever since. It is only as God intervenes in our lives that we can be delivered from the tactics of this powerful invisible foe that we face.

The good news is that God has not left us defenseless. From God's Word in the Bible we learn that He has appointed angels to minister on our behalf and do battle against Satan and his demons. God has provided His own Son, Messiah Jesus, to intercede and fight on our behalf. God has also provided some spiritual armor and weapons with which each follower of Christ can be equipped in order to stand and fight back against this powerful foe. It is only through developing our spiritual eyesight by the power of God's Holy Spirit that we are able to become aware and begin to use this equipment effectively.

As Paul concludes his letter to the church at Ephesus, he emphasizes the importance of being spiritually aware. His teaching continues along the lines of what he has prayed for every believer. The prayer as he stated in Ephesians chapter one is that the God and Father of our Lord Jesus Christ may give us the spirit of wisdom and revelation in the knowledge of Him and that our spiritual eyes of understanding would be enlightened.

Paul wants to help us see the unseen powers at work in the spiritual realm. He wants us to realize what powers work against us. He wants us to understand Christ's surpassing great power that works for us and is available to us. He wants us to realize the spiritual equipment God has provided to enable us to stand and fight back.

Look at how Paul describes it as he concludes this letter:

Ephesians 6:10-18 "NKJV™"
10 Finally, my brethren, be strong in the Lord and in the power of His might.
11 Put on the whole armor of God, that you may be able to stand against the wiles of the devil.
12 For we do not wrestle against flesh and blood, but against principalities, against powers, against the rulers of the darkness of this age, against spiritual hosts of wickedness in the heavenly places.
13 Therefore take up the whole armor of God, that you may be able to withstand in the evil day, and having done all, to stand.
14 Stand therefore, having girded your waist with truth, having put on the breastplate of righteousness,
15 and having shod your feet with the preparation of the gospel of peace;
16 above all, taking the shield of faith with which you will be

able to quench all the fiery darts of the wicked one.
17 And take the helmet of salvation, and the sword of the
Spirit, which is the word of God;
18 praying always with all prayer and supplication in the Spirit,
being watchful to this end with all perseverance and
supplication for all the saints—

Paul uses imagery of a Roman soldier equipped
with protective armor and weapons ready for battle.
He uses this analogy to help us see the spiritual
defenses and weaponry God has equipped us with
through the power and protection of Jesus Christ.

He states in verse ten of chapter six, "Finally my
brethren, be strong in the Lord and in the power of
His might." This is a key concept to understand. If
we try to fight this spiritual battle by our own
strength and power we will fail. But with the power
of Christ working on our behalf in our lives, we
cannot lose because His power is greater than the
enemy. When you receive Jesus Christ into your life,
His Holy Spirit regenerates your spirit (Titus 3:4-7),
He indwells your spirit (John 15:4, 1 Corinthians
3:16-19, Romans 8:11) and gives you eternal life.
With Christ's power at work in our lives we have a
promise from God which the apostle John reassures
us with. "Greater is He that is in you, than he that is
in the world." (1 John 4:4 KJV) John is referring to
Christ's Holy Spirit working in us as believers which

is much greater than Satan's power at work in the world.

Just as a soldier has authority given him by the commander and has equipment for battle provided by the country for whom he fights, so in Christ Jesus we have been given authority and spiritual equipment to stand and fight against the spiritual forces opposed to Christ.

The Breastplate Of Righteousness

As Paul identifies the spiritual armor which God provides for us, he mentions "the breastplate." The breastplate is the piece of armor that protects the vital organs of a soldier such as the heart and lungs. Paul calls our spiritual armor "the breastplate of righteousness." This is an important metaphor. Satan will attack by shooting his ammunition directly at our heart to condemn us. He fires bullets of accusation, anger, jealousy, covetousness, lust and guilt at this area of our lives every day. He wants to discourage us to the point that we will give up trying to follow or serve God. He wants to entice our hearts into rebellion against God's plan for us and God's ways of living. He attacks our feelings because Satan knows how influential our feelings about ourselves and others can be. The only way our hearts can be protected is to know that we have the security of Christ's righteousness standing in our place and for our protection. Paul wrote several times about this spiritual truth which is recorded in the New Testament. Here are some examples:

Romans 3:21-26 "NKJV™"
21 But now the righteousness of God apart from the law is revealed, being witnessed by the Law and the Prophets,
22 even the righteousness of God, through faith in Jesus Christ, to all and on all who believe. For there is no difference;
23 for all have sinned and fall short of the glory of God,
24 being justified freely by His grace through the redemption that is in Christ Jesus,
25 whom God set forth as a propitiation by His blood, through faith, to demonstrate His righteousness, because in His forbearance God had passed over the sins that were previously committed,
26 to demonstrate at the present time His righteousness, that He might be just and the justifier of the one who has faith in Jesus.

God's Word in The New Testament teaches that it is faith in Christ that makes us righteous in the sight of God. God provided Christ to take the punishment for our guilt of sin, and He provided Christ's perfect righteousness for our benefit. Remember 2 Corinthians 5:21? God made Christ who knew no sin, to become sin for us, that we might be made the righteousness of God in Him. Our righteousness before God comes only through what Jesus Christ has done for us. His righteousness is credited to our account when we trust and believe in what Jesus did for us personally through His death on the cross and His resurrection. In this way none of us can brag about how good we are, but instead we acknowledge how good Christ is on our behalf! This becomes our line of defense and our breastplate to protect our hearts. Knowing this truth defends our hearts from the accusations and fiery arrows that the devil fires at us every day.

Here is another example in 1 Corinthians 1:26-31 of what Paul writes about our righteousness being provided for us by Christ alone.

1 Corinthians 1:26-31 (ESV)
26 For consider your calling, brothers: not many of you were wise according to worldly standards, not many were powerful, not many were of noble birth.
27 But God chose what is foolish in the world to shame the wise; God chose what is weak in the world to shame the strong;
28 God chose what is low and despised in the world, even things that are not, to bring to nothing things that are,
29 so that no human being might boast in the presence of God.
30 He is the source of your life in Christ Jesus, whom God made our wisdom and our righteousness and sanctification and redemption.
31 Therefore, as it is written, "Let the one who boasts, boast in the Lord."

Paul mentions this truth in several other of his New Testament writings. In Philippians 1:10 he prays that believers would be filled with the fruit of

righteousness that comes through faith in Jesus
Christ. (See Philippians 1:9-11). In Romans 1:16-17 he
boldly states that he is not ashamed of the gospel of
Jesus Christ because in it the righteousness of God is
revealed by faith in Jesus Christ. He reminds us that
even the Old Testament teaches that the righteous
shall live by faith in God.

In his letter to Titus he describes how this
righteousness should be lived out in ways that honor
God and helps others.

Titus 3:3-8 (ESV)
3 For we ourselves were once foolish, disobedient, led astray,
slaves to various passions and pleasures, passing our days in
malice and envy, hated by others and hating one another.
4 But when the goodness and loving kindness of God our
Savior appeared,
5 he saved us, not because of works done by us in
righteousness, but according to his own mercy, by the washing
of regeneration and renewal of the Holy Spirit,
6 whom he poured out on us richly through Jesus Christ our
Savior,
7 so that being justified by his grace we might become heirs
according to the hope of eternal life.
8 The saying is trustworthy, and I want you to insist on these
things, so that those who have believed in God may be careful
to devote themselves to good works. These things are
excellent and profitable for people.

It is wonderful to know we have Christ's
righteousness living in our hearts as we trust and
follow Him by faith! We can confidently do good

works because of Christ's goodness in us. The apostle John writes in 1 John 3:21 that if our heart does not condemn us, we have confidence before God. However, a heart that does not believe in the righteousness of Christ working on our behalf will lead us to fall away from the living God. We are warned in Hebrews 3:12 not to have an unbelieving heart. This is one of the main reasons the heart is a target for the devil. Our defense is faith in what Jesus Christ has done for us. We can have confidence in Christ's forgiveness and power working on our behalf! Hebrews 4:14-16 reminds us of this powerful truth:

Hebrews 4:14-16 (ESV)
14 Since then we have a great high priest who has passed through the heavens, Jesus, the Son of God, let us hold fast our confession.
15 For we do not have a high priest who is unable to sympathize with our weaknesses, but one who in every respect has been tempted as we are, yet without sin.
16 Let us then with confidence draw near to the throne of grace, that we may receive mercy and find grace to help in time of need.

When the devil attacks your thoughts by reminding you of past sins or telling you how worthless you should feel, remind him of how good Christ Jesus is and what Jesus has done to forgive you and help you. Let the righteousness of Jesus

Christ protect your heart from the ammunition of accusation that Satan fires your way. Romans 10:17 tells us that faith comes by hearing and learning the Word of God. As we hear and read the Word of God, faith begins to take root and grow in our minds. As we meditate on God's Word and apply it to our lives by faith, we become more spiritually mature and able to fight back in this battle.

The Helmet Of Salvation

We need to have our minds protected. A soldier needs a helmet to shield his or her head in battle. A head wound can do major damage toward incapacitating a soldier. In the same way, as followers of Christ we need to have our minds protected from the attacks of Satan. This is why Paul identifies "the helmet of salvation" as another very important piece of spiritual armor that we need to keep in place as we are engaged in this spiritual warfare.

As the control center for the rest of our body, our brain is vital. Paul uses the imagery of a soldier's helmet to help us see the importance of protecting our mind and our thoughts from Satan's attacks. Paul equates "the knowledge of salvation" as a helmet that protects our intellect against the devil's attacks. This is why it is so important to fill your mind with knowledge and understanding of what

Jesus Christ has done for you in order to provide eternal salvation.

The devil will attempt to assail you with doubts and all kinds of disturbing thoughts. Having the knowledge of salvation firmly set in your intellect will help you guard your mind from the effects of the negative thoughts Satan will try to get you to dwell upon. Paul gives some further insight into how to protect your mind in Philippians 4:6-8. Notice in verse seven that Jesus Christ and the peace of God are available to guard your heart and mind when you come to Him in prayer.

Philippians 4:6-8 "NKJV™"
6 Be anxious for nothing, but in everything by prayer and supplication, with thanksgiving, let your requests be made known to God;
7 and the peace of God, which surpasses all understanding, will guard your hearts and minds through Christ Jesus.
8 Finally, brethren, whatever things are true, whatever things are noble, whatever things are just, whatever things are pure, whatever things are lovely, whatever things are of good report, if there is any virtue and if there is anything praiseworthy— meditate on these things.

Try not to think about a big red lollipop. What did you just think of? Probably a big red lollipop! It's not enough just to try and not think about temptation, sin and doubts in our lives. When we try not to think about doubts, that's probably all we will think about. What we need to do is focus on working for Jesus Christ. Focus on doing the things Jesus wants us to do in serving others. Focus on the many ways that God's word teaches us about His love for us. If you occupy your mind with what is good right and true as Philippians 4:8 says, you are much less likely to have room for the devil to fill your mind with negative, discouraging or bad thoughts. It's tough to add doubts to a mind that's full of faith and actively engages in putting God's principles into practice each day. How do you get a mind full of faith? Do what you can to serve the Lord. Meditate on the Word of God and the promises of God offered to us through His Son, Jesus Christ! Fill your mind with positive things and it's a lot tougher for negative things to enter.

The Belt Of Truth

Paul uses another metaphor to describe another important piece of equipment in our spiritual armor. He says in Ephesians 6:14 that we need to be "girded with truth." What does that mean? In the original Greek texts the phrase is "perizonnumi en aletheia." It gives the picture of a soldier wrapping a belt around his waist or hip area in order to hold all of the pieces of armor together to keep them from coming loose or falling off. It gives a picture of fastening garments with a girdle or wide belt. The

Greek word "aletheia" used in this verse means objective truth. That which is true in any matter under consideration. That which is in opposition to corrupt opinions and precepts of false teachers. [5]

The truth of God holds us together. It holds all of our spiritual armor in place as we stand against the deceitful tricks and tactics of the devil. All truth is God's truth. Jesus refers to Himself as the truth. Don't be afraid to seek the truth and stand in the truth.

Marching Boots

Mobility is key in any military battalion. Every good soldier needs to have protection for their feet so they can move swiftly and confidently over any terrain. This is the analogy that Paul uses in verse fifteen where he says to have your feet shod with the preparation of the gospel of peace. He is talking about the importance of followers of Christ being spiritually ready to go anywhere at any time in any situation to spread the good news of Jesus. It is the message of peace with God through faith in Christ

[5]Strong, James: *The Exhaustive Concordance of the Bible : Showing Every Word of the Test of the Common English Version of the Canonical Books, and Every Occurence of Each Word in Regular Order*. electronic ed. Ontario : Woodside Bible Fellowship., 1996, S. H0

which is in opposition to the message of Satan which promotes rebellion against Christ. There are many people who have not yet heard the gospel. There are many who have been spiritually blinded and deceived by Satan. There are many who are still under the oppressive influence of the devil. Christ has given us our marching orders to go everywhere and proclaim the good news of peace with God through the atoning work of Jesus and the power of His Holy Spirit. It is this power that delivers us from Satan's oppression.

The Sword Of The Spirit

Fighting a war can't be all defensive. There must be offensive weaponry available with which we can fight back and even advance against the enemy. So it is with spiritual warfare. Our most effective offensive weapon is what Paul calls in Ephesians six verse seventeen, "the sword of the spirit which is the word of God."

The Word of God recorded in the Bible is our most effective weapon to use in fighting against Satan's tactics of temptation, deceit and confusion. Jesus used the written and spoken Word of God to fight back against Satan when the devil tried to tempt him in the wilderness after Christ's public water baptism. You can read the account in

Matthew chapter four and Luke chapter four. The devil can't stand against God's word of truth.

The Bible says in Hebrews chapter four verse twelve that "the word of God is living and active, sharper than any two edged sword..." It is living and powerful because it is inspired and filled by the Spirit of the living God. Paul instructs in 2 Timothy 3:16 that all scripture is inspired by God and is useful for teaching, correcting and for instruction in right living. When Satan tries to fill your mind with doubts, lies and distortions, go to the Word of God to read it, meditate on it, and apply it to your life. Talk about it with believers. Speak it out loud when you are facing demonic attacks. Pray God's Word in the power of His Holy Spirit. Stand firm in God's promises to you in Christ. The Word of God is our most effective weapon against Satan's deceit.

The Shield Of Faith

Paul describes faith in Jesus Christ as a mighty shield with which we can protect ourselves from the fiery arrows that the devil and his demons launch at us. The Greek word Paul uses for shield in verse sixteen of Ephesians chapter six is "thureos" which is a large oblong, four cornered shield. It was sized to protect a good portion of the person holding it. This shield was large enough that when several soldiers stood close together, each with a thureos side by side, they could form somewhat of a wall of defense against adversarial attacks. This gives us a picture of what it means to be in fellowship with others who share faith in Christ with us. As we stand together side by side, we are better able to help defend each other as a collective against the assault of the enemy.

The Communications Line

In warfare communication is imperative. The troops need to be in touch with their commanding officer for instruction, encouragement and for calling in reinforcements when needed. Paul concludes this section on spiritual warfare by reminding believers in Christ about the most important power of communication with God that we have. It is wireless communication. It is prayer! He writes in verse eighteen of Ephesians chapter six that we should pray always with supplication. Supplication means seeking, asking, entreating as we are led by God's Holy Spirit to pray. He instructs us that we need to persevere in watchful prayer for each other as followers of Christ in this epic spiritual war we are engaged in.

SOME THINGS TO THINK ABOUT

What about you? Can you see the unseen? Do you realize the war that is raging all around you? Which side are you cooperating with? Are you using the spiritual armor that God has provided? Are you in communication with the Lord through prayer, and listening to His instructions through His living Word? Are your feet ready to travel over any terrain in any situation in order to share the message of Christ with others? Are your heart and head protected with the knowledge of salvation and faith in Christ's righteousness? Do you know the Word of God well enough to fight back against the deceptive words of the devil? In what ways have you seen evidence of spiritual battles taking place recently? How have you seen God's Spirit at work in the midst of those battles?

Your effectiveness in winning the battles you are facing now or will face in the future are dependent on how well you utilize the spiritual resources God has provided for you to stand and fight against our adversary the devil.

God has given us a glimpse in Revelation of the end of this spiritual war. Satan will be defeated and put away once and for all. Until that day, we are to live, serve and stand in the power of Christ.

Chapter 7

Keeping Your Spiritual Eyes Open

Paul began his letter to the church at Ephesus with a powerful and encouraging greeting. "Grace be to you, and peace, from God our Father, and from the Lord Jesus Christ."

Paul concludes his letter with similar words:

Ephesians 6:23-24 (KJV)
23 Peace be to the brethren, and love with faith, from God the Father and the Lord Jesus Christ.
24 Grace be with all them that love our Lord Jesus Christ in sincerity. Amen.

God's grace is the concept that forms the bookends for the start and finish of this letter. We can only enjoy forgiveness from God and an ongoing relationship with Him by His grace provided through His Son Jesus Christ. Paul had experienced the grace of God beyond measure in his life. As a former persecutor of the church who tormented and punished followers of Christ, he knew that he deserved God's wrath and punishment. Yet God had extended grace to Paul through Jesus, the very One that Paul was fighting against.

Paul had his spiritual eyes of understanding enlightened when Christ appeared to him. You can read this account in Acts chapter nine. This experience changed Paul's life forever.

As Paul continued to grow in faith and have his spiritual eyes of understanding develop, he was prompted to pray for other believers. Paul had come to know the hope of his calling in Jesus. He had come understand what are the riches of the glorious inheritance he shared with the saints in Christ. He had come to realize the incomparably great power that God was working toward him and in him as a believer. Paul had turned his potential energy of faith into kinetic energy of service for Christ's glory in the world. He understood the importance of having healthy relationships in family and work settings and especially in the church. He also understood the spiritual warfare that is occurring in the world and what God has provided to equip and protect us in the battles we face.

Paul's desire was for believers in Christ to fully come to know these truths. He prayed that our spiritual eyesight would be developed so that we might clearly see what God has provided for us through His Son Jesus, and that we would respond appropriately with active service and gratitude.

Peter was another apostle who also referenced the three major themes that Paul prayed we might understand. Peter mentions the living hope, the rich inheritance and the power that God works toward us in Christ. Peter wrote the following words of encouragement that certainly apply to us today as believers. See if you can find the themes of hope, inheritance, and power mentioned in 1 Peter 1:3-5.

1 Peter 1:3-9 "NKJV™"
3 Blessed be the God and Father of our Lord Jesus Christ,
who according to His abundant mercy has begotten us again
to a living hope through the resurrection of Jesus Christ from
the dead,
4 to an inheritance incorruptible and undefiled and that does
not fade away, reserved in heaven for you,
5 who are kept by the power of God through faith for salvation
ready to be revealed in the last time.
6 In this you greatly rejoice, though now for a little while, if
need be, you have been grieved by various trials,
7 that the genuineness of your faith, being much more
precious than gold that perishes, though it is tested by fire,
may be found to praise, honor, and glory at the revelation of
Jesus Christ,
8 whom having not seen you love. Though now you do not
see Him, yet believing, you rejoice with joy inexpressible and
full of glory,
9 receiving the end of your faith—the salvation of your souls.

Notice in verse eight that Peter is specifically
writing this letter to believers in Jesus Christ who
have not yet seen him with their physical eyes. That
includes us today! Though we have not seen Jesus
with our physical eyes, we have had our spiritual
eyes of understanding illumined enough to recognize
Him through the eyes of faith. We have come to see
and believe by the power of His Holy Spirit at work
in the world and in our hearts and minds. We have
seen Jesus at work through sincere believers who are
bearing the fruit of His Holy Spirit in their lives.

I am thankful for the followers of Jesus who
have displayed these characteristics of love, joy,

peace, patience, kindness, goodness, gentleness, faith and self control in their lives as they have proclaimed the gospel message through word and deed.

Don't be discouraged if you haven't fully grasped all of these concepts. Your spiritual eyesight is still under development. Keep praying, seeking, trusting, and looking to Jesus Christ by faith. That's what Hebrews 12:1-2 encourages us to do.

Hebrews 12:1-2 (ESV)
1 Therefore, since we are surrounded by so great a cloud of witnesses, let us also lay aside every weight, and sin which clings so closely, and let us run with endurance the race that is set before us,
2 looking to Jesus, the founder and perfecter of our faith, who for the joy that was set before him endured the cross, despising the shame, and is seated at the right hand of the throne of God.

As a spiritually born again believer in Jesus Christ I have felt compelled to write this book to share what I have learned. With that in mind I admit that my spiritual eyesight is still under development. Though Christ has opened my spiritual eyes and I am growing in understanding and spiritual perception, I know there is still more I have yet to see. I am reminded of a phrase in another one of Paul's letters in 1 Corinthians 13:12 where he humbly states "For now we see through a glass, darkly; but then face to face: now I know in part; but then shall I know even as also I am known."

We need to pray for each other as Paul prayed. We need to keep our spiritual eyes open and on Jesus as we study God's Word in the Bible. We are reminded in verse six of Philippians chapter one that God will be faithful to complete this good work He has begun in us through Jesus Christ our Lord. May the Lord continue to grant to us the spirit of wisdom and revelation in the knowledge of Him!